The Practice of Philosophy
A Handbook for Beginners

THIRD EDITION

Jay F. Rosenberg
UNIVERSITY OF NORTH CAROLINA
AT CHAPEL HILL

Prentice Hall Upper Saddle River, New Jersey 07458

Library of Congress Cataloging–in–Publication Data

Rosenberg, Jay F.
    The practice of philosophy : a handbook for beginners / Jay F.
Rosenberg.—3rd ed.
        p.   cm.
    Includes bibliographical references.
    ISBN 0-13-230848-7
    1. Philosophy—Introductions.   I. Title
BD21.R644 1996
101—dc20   95-12865
                                                                    CIP

Acquisition editor: Ted Bolen
Manufacturing buyer: Lynn Pearlman
Cover art: *Striped Spheres and Land by Mountains*, Eric Medla/The Image Bank
Editorial assistant: Meg McGuane

© 1996, 1984, 1976 Prentice Hall, Inc.
Simon & Schuster/A Viacom Company
Upper Saddle River, New Jersey 07458

Printed in the United States of America

10 9 8 7 6 5 4 3 2 1

ISBN 0-13-230848-7

Prentice-Hall International (UK) Limited, *London*
Prentice-Hall of Australia Pty. Limited, *Sydney*
Prentice-Hall Canada Inc., *Toronto*
Prentice-Hall Hispanoamericana, S.A., *Mexico*
Prentice-Hall of India Private Limited, *New Delhi*
Prentice-Hall of Japan, Inc., *Tokyo*
Simon & Schuster Asia Pte. Ltd., *Singapore*
Editora Prentice-Hall do Brasil Ltda., *Rio de Janeiro*

DEDICATION

Originally the dedication said: "In a few years she's going to ask me, 'Daddy, just what is it that philosophers do anyway?' Well, that's a long story. Fortunately she can read."

Well, she's all grown up now, and perhaps she's already figured it out—but this one is still for my daughter, Leslie Johanna.

MOTTO

The crux of a philosophical argument often appears to be a Dedekind cut between a series of 'as I will show's and a series of 'as I have shown's. In a sense the preliminaries *are* the argument, and there is no crux apart from their perspicuous deployment. A few more introductory remarks, therefore, and my job will be done.

— WILFRID SELLARS
Science and Metaphysics

Contents

Preface

In three days (as I write this preface), the fall semester of what will be my twenty-ninth year as a professional educator will begin, and I shall once again face the challenge of teaching the most difficult course in our curriculum, Introduction to Philosophy. Since, as I have always believed, there's no substitute for the real thing, I will ask my students to read, think about, and discuss something by Plato and something by Descartes and something by Hume or Berkeley (or perhaps a more contemporary work), and I'll ask them to write a number of short philosophical essays about some of what they've been reading. Most of them, as I have learned during the past twenty-eight years, will find these modest tasks extraordinarily difficult. Most of them initially won't have any clear idea of what's wanted of them or how to begin to cope with philosophical reading and philosophical writing. Most of them will need a good bit of help. Well, that's why there's a teacher in the classroom. Over the years, I have in fact figured out some serviceable ways of explaining things, some moderately effective strategies for helping students get started with the real thing. A while ago, as is my custom when I figure something out, I began to *write these strategies down*. This little book contains most of them. Welcome to my vicarious classroom.

Way back in 1976, in the first edition, I compared this book to a seedling. What motivated the comparison was a remark of William Arrowsmith's regarding the matter of pedagogy in higher education:

> At present the universities are as uncongenial to teaching as the Mojave Desert to a clutch of Druid priests. If you want to restore a Druid priesthood, you cannot do it by offering prizes for Druid-of-the-year. If you want Druids, you must grow forests. There is no other way of setting about it.

By the second edition, eight years later, I judged that the book had grown to be a sapling—but the state of teaching in American universities, alas, was still pretty bleak. And here I am today, eleven years further down the road, embarking on a third edition … and darned if things haven't gotten better! At least at the university where I hang out, teaching is nowadays taken very seriously indeed—so seriously, in fact, that actual *fiscal resources* have been made available in support of it. Imagine that! Meanwhile, *The Practice of Philosophy* has grown into a hardy little evergreen, and it has even germinated—or, more precisely, German-ated (Sorry, I couldn't resist that)—spawning a healthy little *Tannenbaum* named *Philosophieren* ("philosophizing").

So why a third edition? There's only one legitimate reason … I've got something new to say. In the thirteen years since I produced the second edition, I've taught introductory philosophy at least ten more times. It turns out that if you do it often enough, and if you pay attention, you just can't help occasionally stumbling across this or that potentially helpful new pedagogical idea—some improved wording, an illuminating distinction, or a practical piece of advice. Accumulate enough of them and you've got the stuff of which new editions are made. So, as befits its tree metaphor, the book has again grown some fresh branches. In particular, there are two new chapters—one intended to help students avoid some of the conceptual pitfalls relating to *modifiers,* especially the slippery modal adverbs, and one illustrating techniques for probing beneath the expository surface of a given question to uncover the inevitable structure of presuppositions and problems underlying it. I've also taken the occasion to engage in a bit of *topiary,* working through the entire earlier text in careful detail. In consequence, parts of it have been rewritten in the interest of greater clarity; parts have been augmented with additional useful materials; and parts have been relocated, reordered, and restructured to provide a smoother and more natural exposition. All in all, it's still the same old tree, but it's been shaped up a bit to make it tidier, more accessible, and (I hope) even more beneficial to its pedagogical clientele. Happy climbing!

Jay F. Rosenberg
Chapel Hill, North Carolina

Prospect

This handbook is meant to serve two purposes. The more practical purpose is to give beginning students of philosophy some helpful suggestions for approaching an intellectual enterprise which will probably initially strike them as thoroughly bizarre. To a typical beginner, philosophical practices often seem arbitrary, pointless, and trivial—and yet, at the same time, surprisingly difficult and indescribably frustrating. The second and more important purpose of this handbook is to try to explain why this happens, what it is about philosophy that produces these appearances.

Philosophy, in fact, differs significantly from almost all other academic disciplines currently populating our universities. How and why it is different is the focus of my less practical but more important theme. Since it *is* different, however, a course of studies in philosophy will inevitably make different demands on students from those imposed by other academic studies. The nature of these different demands and how to begin to meet them—a small kit of helpful hints about how to *do* it—is my more practical theme. There's a third thing that I would like to be able to pass on in this book, but I don't think I can. It's the genuine sense of liberation, satisfaction, and even joy that can be reached through the practice of philosophy. That is something each of us must find or fail to find on his or her own. The most I can realistically hope for is that whatever I *do* succeed in communicating here will perhaps make it a little easier to find.

A few cautionary notes are probably in order. First, this handbook is largely concerned with technique. In consequence, sad to say, it is likely to be rather dry. Original, visionary philosophical writing is rewarding in exciting ways, but this book bears about the same relation to original visionary philosophical writing that a carpentry shop manual bears to a finely crafted Chippendale chair. Reading this sort of handbook isn't what produces the sense of liberation, satisfaction, and joy that I spoke of a moment ago, any more than reading carpentry manuals makes beautiful chairs. What does the trick—if you're lucky—is *mastering* the techniques described in the shop manual and putting them into action. And not only is that more difficult, but you're also likely to make quite a few mistakes along the way. Chippendale's *first* chair was probably a wobbly disaster.

A second sad consequence of emphasizing technique is that one rather quickly reaches the limits of what's teachable. The hard truth of the matter is that there just isn't any teachable technique for creation or discovery or insight or understanding.

You can teach someone how to look, but not how to see; how to search, but not how to find. The topics of this handbook are the things that might be teachable—organization and exegesis, exposition and argument—techniques for processing conceptual raw materials. The raw materials of critical or constructive insight themselves, however, will have to come from somewhere outside all this technique. Critical acumen and creative originality can't be taught. At best they can be nourished, enhanced, and ripened. But for that, just two things have been found to help: familiarity with the lay of the land, and beyond that, practice, practice, and more practice. Both take time and self-discipline. To gain familiarity, there is no substitute for extensive reading; to gain practice, no substitute for extensive writing. This handbook does not provide the reading. It is rather meant to supplement such materials. The best things to write about, correlatively, are likely to be the things that you are reading; but I have supplied an appendix to this handbook with a handful of puzzles and passages that are meant to provide or suggest topics suitable for beginning philosophical writing.

A third, rather different sort of cautionary note concerns the *style* of philosophizing that has shaped this handbook. There are at present two main philosophical styles at large in the Western world, falling roughly on opposite sides of the English Channel. The Anglo-American style is often characterized as "analytic" or "linguistic"; the Continental style as "existentialist" or "phenomenological." These are, of course, loose and untidy groupings. Practitioners of both styles can be found everywhere, and the styles themselves intermingle—philosophy for the "Chunnel"—and shade off into large gray areas not usefully branded with any single label. But this handbook is centered firmly in the analytic style of philosophizing. The kinds of issues, problems, and questions it regards as appropriate to raise and the types of answers it advocates and illustrates are conditioned by and reflect this fundamental stylistic orientation. There's nothing wrong with that—some stylistic decision or other is unavoidable—but it bears mentioning, especially in an introductory work, that there are perfectly respectable alternatives.

The choice of a philosophical style is only one of the individual commitments shaping this handbook. Every book has an author. In consequence, no matter how abstract or routine the subject matter or how dry and sterilized the academic prose, every book is conditioned by some individual's idiosyncrasies, prejudices presuppositions, and ideological biases—if in no other way then, at least, by its author's choices of what to include and what to omit. This book is no exception. It didn't write itself; *I* wrote it. Like most authors, I am a typically complex person. I come fully equipped with beliefs, desires, competences, ideals, preferences, goals, intentions, and values. Some of this equipment controls what goes on in this handbook. Of course it does. I am convinced that the commitments which do so are shared and useful and rationally defensible. (That they *should* be, of course, is one of those values I was just talking about.) If this were, for instance, a mathematics text, it might not be necessary to mention such matters. They would go without saying. In philosophy, however, there is a point to making them explicit. What I want to turn to next is some of the reasons why this is so.

The Philosophical Impulse and Where It Leads

At this point, you are doubtless expecting to find a definition of the word 'philosophy', an explanation of the subject matter of philosophy, some statement beginning "Philosophy is the study of . . ." Well, one of the peculiarities of philosophy is that it is at best extremely difficult, and at worst impossible, to characterize it in subject-matter terms by giving a useful compact description of what it is about. To put it paradoxically, philosophy is, in its own fashion, about everything. Shortly I shall try to explain this cryptic remark, but there are some things that need to be said first.

Philosophy is, of course, something in which people engage. It is a practice or activity, something people do. And unlike, for instance, digging ditches or playing the fiddle, the practice of philosophy is fundamentally an activity of reason. By itself, however, this says very little, for any number of characteristically human practices are activities of reason. Literature and history and science are all surely activities of reason, but philosophy is neither literature nor history nor science—although it may be literary or historical or even, in an extended sense, scientific. Practicing philosophers typically present their thoughts in written form, but their first order of business is not creative literary expression. They often discuss the views of their historical predecessors in their historical settings, but their first order of business is not the scholarly sorting through of historical materials. And they often advance explanations and theories, but their theorizing is not grounded in and accountable to controlled observation and experiment in the way that the theorizing of scientists is. What, then, is the proper business of philosophers?

Let me try to remind you of something. At one time or another, almost everyone has experienced a certain impulse, and it's likely that you have too. Typically it comes as a feeling, an intrusion in the everyday routine, a sort of wonderment or unsettling. And often it resolves itself into a vague but suggestive question: Do space and time go on forever? What if there isn't any God? (Or: What if there *is*?) Is anyone genuinely free? Is anything ever really right or wrong? Are there any absolute truths? Can some works of art really be better than others? And, of course: What is the meaning of life? This is the sort of feeling that Aristotle had in mind when he remarked that philosophy begins in wonder. However inarticulate, the disturbing sense that there is an important gap in one's understanding of things, a big question that still needs to be answered, is precisely an impulse toward philosophical activity.

Few people go beyond this point. The reason, quite simply, is that they don't know *how* to go beyond it. How does one think about such things? *Can* one think about such things? Perhaps it is just impossible to go beyond this point. The mind boggles. One's thinking flounders, stumbles in circles, grows cramped and knotted. Eventually the moment passes—or is made to pass. Somehow the question gets dismissed. It is postponed or rejected or repressed. And yet the feeling often remains, the frustrating sense that these are after all important questions, questions with important answers. If only one knew how to find those answers!

A practicing philosopher is, among other things, a person who tries to find them. It is part of the proper business of practicing philosophers to get beyond such inchoate feelings and to bring these vague, suggestive, big questions within the scope of an activity of reason, to move them out of the heart and into the mind. It is part of a philosopher's job to transform such questions into something that one can think about—and then to think about them. For such an undertaking, philosophers must have both a general strategy—a method—and particular tactics—techniques for applying that method. And so they do. Philosophy is an activity of reason with its own strategy and its own tactics, its own method and techniques. It is, in short, a *discipline*.

One of the initially most striking features of the philosophical discipline is its academic fragmentation into a multiplicity of diverse *philosophies of* other disciplines. Thus one finds courses of study offered in philosophy of science, philosophy of art, philosophy of religion, philosophy of mathematics, of history, of psychology, of law, of language, and so on through the whole catalog of human intellectual endeavors. Philosophy thus takes on the character of a sort of "second-order" discipline, one which, in some sense, can be about the "first-order" activities of scientists, artists, theologians, mathematicians, historians, psychologists, jurists, linguists, and their many colleagues. If one were to insist on characterizing philosophy in subject-matter terms, one would then need a very broad subject-matter description indeed, something along the lines of "the rational, cognitive, or conceptual activities of persons." Seen in this light, philosophy as an activity is the application of reason to its own operations, the rational study of rational practices. It is in this way that philosophy comes, in its own fashion, to be about everything.

Seen in this light, in fact, philosophy also comes to be about itself. Since it is itself an activity of reason, philosophy falls within the scope of its own field of study; and, indeed, there exists the philosophy of philosophy (*meta*-philosophical inquiry) as well. "What is a proper philosophical question?" and "What is appropriate philosophical methodology?" are themselves two fine examples of proper philosophical questions. And this is yet another reason that it is difficult or even impossible to give a useful compact description of the proper subject-matter of philosophical study. Any such description, including the one I have just given, is itself the expression of a philosophical thesis, position, or view.[1]

---

[1] Charles J. Bontempo and S. Jack Odell, eds., *The Owl of Minerva* (New York: McGraw-Hill, 1975) is a fascinating collection of reflective essays by some fifteen contemporary philosophers on the topic: Just what is philosophy anyway?

One can see the philosophical impulse at work in the kinds of "second-order" questions that a practicing philosopher is inclined to ask. One helpful description of such questions divides them into two groups: questions of *meaning* and questions of *justification*. Notably absent from this classification, however, are questions of truth. Practitioners of this or that "first-order" discipline make a variety of interesting claims. A physicist might say, for example, that gases consist of molecules or that every material object is composed of atoms. An art critic might claim that Michelangelo's *David* is a more fully realized work than his *Pieta*. A theologian might assert that God is merciful; an historian, that the underlying causes of World War II were primarily economic; a linguist, that the linguistic competences of human beings cannot be explained without presupposing innate, genetically transmitted linguistic capacities; and so on. Now practicing philosophers will typically not be inclined to ask whether this or that interesting "first-order" claim is in fact true. If pressed, they are likely to decline to answer on the ground that they lack the special expertise of the "first-order" practitioner that is needed to assess the truth or false-hood of such claims. But they may well insist that there is some business which is their proper concern and which needs to be gotten out of the way first.

One sort of question that philosophers in practice may pursue concerns the problem of *understanding* such interesting "first-order" claims. What does it mean to say of one work of art that it is "more fully realized" than another? What are "underlying causes" anyway? Philosophers are constitutionally disinclined to take such claims at face value, not because they are inherently more skeptical than other people, but because they are typically troubled about what the face value of such claims is supposed to be. That gases consist of molecules, for instance, may look like a straightforward enough claim. But does a gas consist of molecules in the same way that a ladder consists of rungs and sides? In the way that a jigsaw puzzle consists of pieces? In the way that a forest consists of trees? In the way that a sentence consists of words? In the way that a cake consists of flour, eggs, sugar, butter, and milk? How can something visible and colored—a chair, for example—be composed entirely of things—for example, atoms—none of which is visible and none of which can be colored?

Again, we understand reasonably well what it is for a parent or a judge to be merciful, but can a theologian who speaks of God as merciful possibly mean what we ordinarily mean? God's mercifulness, after all, is evidently supposed to be com-patible with the existence of disease, drought, famine, war, earthquake, hurricane, tornado, and typhoon, and with all the diverse human sufferings which He apparent-ly allows such calamities to visit indiscriminately upon the innocent and the guilty alike. And that is hardly what we would *ordinarily* expect from a merciful being. Yet again, a philosopher may ask, do we have any intelligible notion of a "linguistic capacity" as something which can be genetically transmitted in the way that eye color, for instance, is genetically transmitted? If we think of the fundamental philo-sophical impulse as expressing a need to make sense of the world and our place in it, we can begin to see how it finds articulate application in the more limited project of making sense of the interesting and provocative, but often puzzling and peculiar, things that practitioners of the various "first-order" disciplines from time to time say about the world and our place in it.

Second, a philosopher may in practice pursue an inquiry into "first-order" practitioners' *entitlement* to make the various interesting claims that they in fact do make, that is, into the grounds—explicit or implicit—that they do or could offer in support of those claims. How can the observable gross behavior of substances, objects, and instruments in the laboratory legitimize physicists' claims about unobservable particles or forces? Can judgments of aesthetic worth somehow be intersubjectively validated, or are they necessarily nothing more than expressions of personal taste? Does it ultimately require an appeal to a special mode of religious experience to secure particular theological claims, and is there—indeed, can there be—such a mode of experience?

What people most frequently think of as *philosophical* questions, matters properly falling within the traditional province of philosophical inquiry, are radical generalizations of such questions. Thus philosophers will typically not ask after the grounds of this or that particular aesthetic judgment, but rather whether judgments of aesthetic worth in general—or, even more broadly, whether *any* judgments of value, aesthetic or moral—admit of objective justification. Nor are they inclined to take for granted the implied contrast between judgments of value and judgments of fact. Whether that distinction can be sensibly drawn, and, if so, in what it consists, is also up for investigation. Again, philosophers will inquire into the legitimacy of *any* inference from the observed to the unobserved, whether what is inferred are the forces and particles of the physicist, the private thoughts and desires of ordinary people, or tomorrow's sunrise. And, of course, the very distinction between what can and cannot be observed itself becomes a theme of philosophical exploration. And yet again, practicing philosophers will want to explore the limitations of perceptual experience in general, not simply as one possible mode of justification for theological beliefs, but as a faculty yielding any knowledge of a world independent of our experiencing it. Or, conversely, they may inquire whether theological claims can be warranted at all, by experience or by reasoning. The practicing philosopher is thus a generalist *par excellence*. As one great twentieth-century practitioner[2] once put it:

> The aim of philosophy, abstractly formulated, is to understand how things in the broadest possible sense of the term hang together in the broadest possible sense of the term.

Whatever the details of its methodology, then, the practice of philosophy—unlike the activities characteristic of the "first-order" disciplines or, for that matter, our daily business in the practical world—is carried on at one remove from the "first-order" facts. In consequence, it is a particularly rarefied and abstract practice. It is not an inquiry into the facts in this sense at all, but into the methods by which we can search for such facts, the legitimate grounds or reasons on the basis of which we can come to assert them, and the concepts we use in formulating and expressing them. My late colleague W.D. Falk once said it this way: Ordinary folk ask "What time is it?" but a philosopher asks "What is time?"

---

[2]   Wilfrid Sellars, in "Philosophy and the Scientific Image of Man," originally published in *Frontiers of Science and Philosophy*, ed. by Robert Colodny (Pittsburgh, PA: University of Pittsburgh Press, 1962).

Recognizing this allows us to explain much of what is peculiar and problematic about the practice of philosophy—the seeming elusiveness and arbitrariness of its methods, its often-lamented lack of a firm direction and of generally accepted concrete results which could be counted as progress, and, more generally, the aura of unreality and detachment which non-philosophers find so strikingly characteristic of the discipline. The root of all these appearances lies in the fact that philosophers are not in any straightforward way thinking about the world. What they are thinking about is *thinking about the world*. Such results as there are, then, do not take the form of new facts but rather, at best, consist in a new clarity about what are and what aren't the old facts, and about their modes of legitimization.

Practicing philosophers are thus the very model of theoreticians and, since the objects of their theorizing are at one remove from the facts, the very opposite of practical folk. The sort of understanding at which a philosopher aims is not a practical understanding, which is a condition of effective action. It is an understanding of the deep presuppositions and preconditions of those "first-order" forms of understanding which can shape our actions. Philosophical inquiry is not instrumental. It is not a tool. Philosophy bakes no bread and builds no bridges. It aims at clarity, not as a means to facilitate action or to advance other independent, life-goals, but simply for the sake of clarity—to understand "how things in the broadest possible sense of the term hang together in the broadest possible sense of the term," and to understand the limits of such understanding. So, although there may be philosophical technique, there is no philosophical technology. That is surely what is meant by the etymological characterization of the philosopher as a lover, not of knowledge (*episteme*) but of wisdom (*sophia*).

I have been speaking of philosophy as a practice which comes after the "first-order" special sciences, an activity which probes the foundations and superstructures of edifices already built. But it is no less correct to think of philosophy as something *prior* to science, as the mother of sciences. "Philosophy begins in wonder," Aristotle said, but this root wonder at the complex world in which we find ourselves, this fundamental philosophical impulse, is ultimately the wellspring from which all human inquiry flows. Speculation and theorizing about change and motion and the stuff of the world long preceded the organized experimental disciplines which we today think of as the physical sciences. Before there were physics and chemistry there was "natural philosophy" (by which name physical science is still sometimes called in England), and our sharper-edged disciplines grew from these speculative philosophical origins as smoothly as an oak from an acorn. People theorized about justice long before there existed any formal discipline of jurisprudence. People explored possible forms of human society and its governance long before sociology and political science became autonomous pursuits. Centuries of speculation about our human capacities to think and know and feel preceded the various empirical studies we now call psychology. And all this theorizing, exploration, and speculation was and is fairly called 'philosophy'. Newton and Einstein, Jefferson and Lenin, Freud and Skinner all dealt no less with problems and puzzles properly thought of as philosophical than did Aristotle and Leibniz, Locke and Hegel, Kant and Hume.

Philosophy still preserves this historical role—at the cutting edge. Philosophy and the special sciences grade off into one another at the speculative margins.

Theoretical physicists and philosophers of physics, political theorists and political philosophers, linguistic theorizers and philosophers of language, theoretical psychologists and philosophers of mind—all of these practitioners share their problems. Given what has already been said about philosophy's "second-order" character, this should not be surprising. For it is precisely on the frontiers of any discipline that the characteristically philosophical concerns of making sense (What does it mean?) and establishing entitlements (How could we tell?) arise with special force and immediacy. The two roles of philosophy—as both a critical study of extant conceptual structures and a speculative source of new ones—complement rather than compete with one another, rounding out the picture of philosophy as our most general intellectual encounter with the nature and limits of human reason in all its manifestations.

The history of philosophy—the great work of past philosophers—has a special role to play in this encounter. One thing you will discover is that a good bit of the ongoing business of a practicing philosopher consists in discussion and evaluation of the views of other philosophers and of the arguments that have been advanced in support of them. This fact has led some critics to speak sarcastically of academic philosophical activity as the treatment of conceptual diseases that philosophers catch only from one another. But it turns out that the special role of philosophy's own history in its proper practice is also a reflection of the "second-order" character of philosophy that I have been describing. Indeed, it will prove worthwhile to take a closer look at the sources of this sort of philosophical "inbreeding."

Two natural scientists may disagree at the level of their theorizing about the proper explanation of a body of observed phenomena, but they share the phenomena themselves as common ground. They may disagree about what a cluster of experimental results *shows*, but they typically do not disagree about what the experimental results *are*. Similarly, two historians may disagree about the interpretation to place on a set of documents, but they share the documents themselves as common ground. They may disagree about what the documents *imply* (e.g., about why something happened when and how it did), but they typically do not disagree about what the documents *say* (about what in fact happened and when it did). And even two disputing theologians, at least those of the same religious persuasion, can find a common ground in their shared faith and, often, in their common commitment to particular sacred texts. So, in the "first-order" disciplines, when disagreement breaks out, there is usually a built-in way for all the parties to a dispute to return to an area of agreement and proceed systematically and afresh from there.

Philosophers, in contrast, share neither phenomena nor experiments, neither documentary data nor faith. They characteristically operate at one remove from the "first-order" facts. What philosophers do share, however, is a *history*, the common conceptual ancestry of their great predecessors. Suppose, for instance, that two contemporary philosophers disagree about the limits of perceptual knowledge, that is, about what it is possible to come to know about the world through sensory experience. It is clear that one thing they cannot do is simply retreat to a shared agreement about what is scientifically known about the physiological and psychological processes of perception. For if physiologists and psychologists know anything about perceptual processes, that knowledge must ultimately rest on observations, on perceptual experiences; whereas what is in dispute between the two philosophers is precisely what *can* be known through perceptual experiences, not just about perceptual processes but about anything at all. Thus, although the two philosophers may agree, for example, about what practicing neurophysiologists *say* about human perceptual processes, their philosophical disagreement infects both the sense of those neurophysiological claims (what to make of them) and their legitimacy. The "second-order" nature of the philosophers' disagreement precisely precludes their finding a shared "neutral ground" in the claims advanced within some "first-order" discipline.

Where the disputing philosophers can find some common ground, however, is in their shared conceptual heritage. For the great philosophers of the past—Plato, Aristotle, Aquinas, Descartes, Berkeley, Hume, Kant, among others—have all taken stands on the limits of perceptual knowledge and have offered arguments in support of their stands. The two disputing philosophers can thus productively relocate their disagreement in their differing attitudes toward and assessments of one or several of these historical stances. In commenting on and critically evaluating the substantive views and supporting arguments offered by their mutually acknowledged predecessors, they can find the beginnings of a process which allows the development of convergent understandings and thereby carries with it, as well, at least the possibility of an ultimate resolution of their initial dispute.

The history of philosophy thus plays a crucial methodological role in the practice of philosophy. It does not enter as a primary *object* of philosophical inquiry, but rather as an indispensable *medium* of that inquiry. It provides philosophers with a common expository idiom, a shared vocabulary of concepts and a collection of paradigms of philosophical reasoning, which can serve as mutual starting points for contemporary re-explorations of central philosophical concerns. This history is a fertile stock of views and supporting considerations, to be sifted and resifted, assessed and reassessed, and—by the best of practicing philosophers—supplemented and enriched.

The historical concerns of practicing philosophers, then, do not end with an understanding of what their predecessors believed. Practicing philosophers always press through to the crucial question of why their predecessors believed what they did, or, better put, the question of why one (why *anyone*) ought to believe it. For the "why" at issue here is not the "why" of, say, psychoanalysis or sociology; it is the "why" of *reasons*. It is with the reasonings of their predecessors, and not with their motivations or the social and historical forces that shaped their views, that practicing philosophers concern themselves. At least in its critical dimension, then, philosophical progress is neither a matter of new facts and forecasts nor one of bread or bombs or bridges. It rather consists in such subtle business as refining one's understanding of a problem, attaining greater argumentative rigor, grasping connections, noticing tacit presuppositions, and even finally seeing the point of a remark.

And just occasionally, if one is sufficiently persistent and especially fortunate, these minute elements can momentarily fall together and interlock into a larger visionary whole. And it is then that you find the sense of liberation and satisfaction and joy of which I earlier spoke.

CHAPTER TWO

Philosophy in Action: A Case Study

O
ur discussion of philosophy has so far been conducted in fairly abstract and general terms. What we need to begin to bring it down to earth, to serve the more practical purpose of this handbook, is a good solid example of philosophical reasoning in action. Let me begin, then, by telling a series of small *stories* which will lead up to a nice philosophical *puzzle*.

For the purpose of these stories, we will suppose that ancient Greek shipwrights were such masters of joinery that an *ancient Greek ship* consisted of exactly one thousand cunningly interlocking wooden planks of various shapes and sizes, *and nothing else*—that is, no nails, screws, pegs, ropes, wires, or the like. This, of course, is pure fiction. It wasn't so. *Actual* ancient Greek ships were doubtless cobbled together in a variety of ways, but as far as I know, none of them consisted only of one thousand cunningly interlocked planks. So what we have here is a case of conceptual "let's pretend" or what philosophers call a *thought-experiment*. I'll have more to say about thought-experiments later. For now, it suffices that the present pretense, so to speak, short-circuits a number of potential *distractions* and helps us concentrate our attention on the essential features of the case.

I want to creep up on my ultimate puzzle by telling two preliminary stories about two imaginary ancient Greek ships. I'll call them the "Pride of Sparta" and the "Maid of Thebes." Our stories also need a shipwright together with his shipyard, fully equipped with two dry-docks, Dock A and Dock B. Let's call that enterprise "Ships-R-Us." Now we're ready for the first two stories.

Story 1: The Pride of Sparta

The owner of the Pride of Sparta brings her ship into Ships-R-Us for a thorough barnacle scraping, and the shipwright parks it in Dock A. Shortly thereafter, however, the shipwright realizes that he needs Dock A free for new construction and decides to move the Pride of Sparta into Dock B. Alas, his heavy lifting crane is out of order. Not to worry. His crack crew can simply *disassemble* the ship in Dock A, one plank at a time, and *reassemble* it in Dock B, plank for plank. Supposing that it takes the crew **t** minutes to move one plank, after 1000**t** minutes the job will be done, and Dock A will be free. And so it comes to pass.

It will help us to envision what is happening in this story if we take a few "snapshots" of the process at its various stages. Let's picture the situation in the shipyard at the beginning, at minute 0, before anything has been done, this way:

At the end of the first **t** minutes, then, after one plank has been moved, the shipyard will look like this:

Jumping ahead to sometime around the halfway point, about 500**t** minutes into the job, what we find in the shipyard now looks more or less like this:

```
        O                           O
       O O                         O O O
        O                           O
      O O O O                       O O O
       O O O                         O O
┌─────────────────────┬─────────────────────┐
│       Dock A        │       Dock B        │
└─────────────────────┴─────────────────────┘
```

Finally, after 1000**t** minutes have elapsed, what we would see in the Ships-R-Us shipyard would be this:

```
                                   O   O
                                  O O O O O
                                   O   O
                                 O O O O O O O
                                  O O O O O
┌─────────────────────┬─────────────────────┐
│       Dock A        │       Dock B        │
└─────────────────────┴─────────────────────┘
```

The Pride of Sparta, we naturally conclude, has been moved from one dry-dock to the other. At minute 0, the ship is in Dock A; at minute 1000**t**, the same ship is in

Dock B. That's what it looks like when an ancient Greek ship is moved from one dock to the other, plank by plank, without using the heavy lifting crane.

Our next story, in contrast, plays out entirely in one dry-dock. It goes like this:

Story 2: The Maid of Thebes

The Maid of Thebes is composed of 1000 weathered and seaworn oak planks. One day her owner decides that the ship could use a complete and thorough *renovation*. He therefore sails the Maid of Thebes into Ships-R-Us, parking her in Dock A as instructed, and gives the shipwright the following order: Please replace all the weathered and seaworn *oak* planks with sound new *teak* planks. Not to worry. The shipwright's crack crew can replace an old oak plank with a new teak plank in **t** minutes, so after 1000t minutes, the job will be done. And so it comes to pass.

Using 'o' to represent an *oak* plank and '+' to represent a *teak* plank, if we take four "snapshots" of the Ships-R-Us shipyard at the same stages of the process described in this story as we did before, our photo album looks like this:

```
Minute                O  O
0                   O O O O O
                      O  O
                  O O O O O O O
                    O O O O O
          ┌─────────────────────────┬─────────────────────────┐
          │         Dock A          │         Dock B          │
          └─────────────────────────┴─────────────────────────┘

Minute                O  O
t                   O O O O O
                      O  O
                  O O O O O O O
                    + O O O
          ┌─────────────────────────┬─────────────────────────┐
          │         Dock A          │         Dock B          │
          └─────────────────────────┴─────────────────────────┘

Minute                +  O
500t                + + + O O
                      +  O
                  + + + + O O O
                    + + + O O
          ┌─────────────────────────┬─────────────────────────┐
          │         Dock A          │         Dock B          │
          └─────────────────────────┴─────────────────────────┘

Minute                +  +
1000t               + + + + +
                      +  +
                  + + + + + + +
                    + + + + +
          ┌─────────────────────────┬─────────────────────────┐
          │         Dock A          │         Dock B          │
          └─────────────────────────┴─────────────────────────┘
```

The Maid of Thebes, we naturally conclude, has received the complete renovation its owner wanted. At minute 0, the ship, composed of seaworn oak planks, is in Dock A; at minute 1000t, the same ship, now composed of new teak planks, is *still* in Dock A. That's what it looks like when an ancient Greek ship is renovated, plank by plank, while remaining parked in one dry-dock.

Now we are ready for our final story. Pay careful attention to what's going on in each of the two dry-docks. There's a question coming up.

Story 3: The Spirit of Athens

The Spirit of Athens is composed of 1000 sound and seaworthy oak planks. One day, however, its owner—Theseus by name—is rather taken by the trim figure cut by the renovated Maid of Thebes. "I'd like to have a teak ship myself," he thinks, and, being a man of action, off to Ships-R-Us he sails. Parking the Spirit of Athens in Dock A as instructed, he tells the shipwright what he wants. "Not to worry," says the shipwright, "My crack crew can get the job done in 1000t hours. Come back after that." But when Theseus has gone, the wily shipwright thinks to himself, "Hmmm. Those are mighty good oak planks. There's no point in letting them go to waste." With this thought in mind, then, he instructs his crew that the oak planks which they are *replacing* with teak planks in dry-dock A should be *reassembled*, plank for plank, in dry-dock B. And so it comes to pass.

This time, our photo album contains the following "snapshots":

Minute 0		
	O O	
	O O O O O	
	O O	
	O O O O O O O	
	O O O O O	
Dock A		**Dock B**

Minute t		
	O O	
	O O O O O	
	O O	
	O O O O O O O	
	+ O O O	O
Dock A		**Dock B**

Minute 500t		
	+ O	O
	+ + + O O	O O O
	+ O	O
	+ + + + O O O	O O O O
	+ + + O O	O O O
Dock A		**Dock B**

	Ship X	*Ship Y*
Minute 1000t	+ + + + + + + + + + + + + + + + + +	○ ○ ○○○○○ ○ ○ ○○○○○○○ ○○○○○
	Dock A	**Dock B**

Unlike Stories 1 and 2, Story 3 ends with *two* ships, one in Dock A—call it *Ship X*—and the other in Dock B—call it *Ship Y*. And now we are finally ready for our puzzle: Which ship, X or Y, if either, is *Theseus's* ship, the Spirit of Athens?

The first thing it's important to be clear about is what kind of question this is. It is *not*, for instance, a question about opinions or expectations, that is, about which ship, X or Y, Theseus is likely to *think* is the Spirit of Athens or which one the shipwright will *say* it is. What we want to know is which ship, X or Y, actually *is* the Spirit of Athens. We don't want to know what Theseus thinks or the shipwright says; we want to know what's *true*. Again, our question is not one about ownership: for example, about which ship, X or Y, an ancient Greek judge would award Theseus in a lawsuit. Judges sometimes get it right, and they sometimes get it wrong—but we know well enough what ship a judge *ought* to award Theseus. A judge *ought* to award Theseus *his* ship, namely, the Spirit of Athens. Our question is: Which one is that?

Our question, in short, is a question about *identification*. We can put it this way: We know where the Spirit of Athens was at minute 0, when Theseus brought it in. It was parked in Dock A. At minute 1000t there's a ship, Ship X, parked in Dock A, but there's also a ship, Ship Y, parked in Dock B. What we want to know now is which ship, X or Y, is the ship that *was* parked in Dock A *at minute 0*. We can locate the Spirit of Athens at minute 0. What we want to be able to do is locate it *again*—to relocate *that very ship*—at minute 1000t. The question is now clear enough. But at minute 1000t we have two candidates, Ship X and Ship Y. How shall we begin?

One way to begin is by surveying the range of *possible* answers to the question and, perhaps, narrowing down the set of "live options" to a manageable number. When students first start to think about this puzzle, what they usually discover is that they have one or another of various possible *opinions*. It is likely, for instance, that some of you think that Ship X is the Spirit of Athens and others that it's Ship Y. As we shall soon see, there is something to be said for each of these answers. But some students are sufficiently baffled by their first encounter with the puzzle that they find themselves drawn to views that are rather less plausible. Some of you, for example, may find the problem of choosing between X and Y so confusing that you are tempted to answer that *neither* Ship X *nor* Ship Y is Theseus's ship, the Spirit of Athens. And some of you may even be desperate enough to entertain the "answer" that *both* X *and* Y are Theseus's ship, the Spirit of Athens. Unfortunately, neither of these alternatives holds up very well under examination.

Indeed, the second of these peculiar "answers" can be dismissed on purely logical grounds. We're trying to locate *one* ship, Theseus's ship, the Spirit of Athens. X and Y, however, are *two* ships—and it's simply impossible for two things to be one thing. Of course, two things can be "the same" or "identical" in the way that, for instance, so-called "identical twins" are "the same" or "identical," namely *exactly alike*; but our two ships X and Y aren't even "the same" or "identical" in this loose manner of speaking. Ship X, after all, is composed entirely of oak planks and Ship Y entirely of teak planks. There is thus simply *no* sense to be made of the proposal that X and Y are both "really" *one and the same* ship, that is, Theseus's ship, the Spirit of Athens.

The proposal that *neither* X *nor* Y is the Spirit of Athens doesn't fare much better. Here, to be sure, nobody is suggesting a logical absurdity. But if we decide to go this route, we do inherit a rather nasty new puzzle, namely: What happened to *Theseus's* ship? If neither X nor Y is the Spirit of Athens, *what has become of the Spirit of Athens*? It seems to have simply disappeared. It is, of course, doubtless possible to tell some ingeniously convoluted story here according to which we were dealing with *three* ships, X and Y and the Spirit of Athens—one of which vanished as the other two came into existence—but, given that there are at least two initially more plausible alternatives, that sort of story should hardly hold much appeal for us.

The upshot, I think, is that we can narrow our set of "live options" down to just two: Either Ship X is Theseus's ship, the Spirit of Athens, or Ship Y is. Each of these answers, it turns out, has considerable initial plausibility. Think of how you might try to convince someone else that one or another of them is correct.

Someone who favors the first answer, that Ship X is Theseus's ship, for instance, might argue as follows:

The Case for Ship X:

It's just like the case of the Maid of Thebes in Story 2. Look at the snapshots of dry-dock A. They're just the same. Theseus brought his ship in for a complete renovation, and it *got* a complete renovation. It was parked in Dock A at minute 0, and—although lots of things were *done to it* while it was there—there it stayed for the whole 1000t minutes. As it happened, there were other things going on in dry-dock B during those 1000t minutes, but that's simply irrelevant to *our* question. What we need to do is to keep track of *Theseus's* ship during those 1000t minutes, and that's easy. *Theseus's* ship was in dry-dock A the whole time, getting a complete renovation. So it's Ship X, the one in Dock A at the end of the procedure, that's Theseus's ship, the Spirit of Athens.

On the other hand, someone who favors the second answer, that Ship Y is Theseus's ship, might offer a rather different set of considerations.

The Case for Ship Y:

It's just like the case of the Pride of Sparta in Story 1. Look at the snapshots of dry-dock B. They're just the same. You'd surely agree, wouldn't you, that if the shipwright had simply *moved* the Spirit of Athens from Dock A to Dock B right at the beginning, say, by using the heavy lifting crane, and then proceeded to *build* a teak ship *just like* Theseus's in dry-dock A, that the Spirit of Athens would be in Dock B at the end of the 1000t minutes. Well, that's more or less what actually happened. Of course, the ship-wright's crew didn't move Theseus's ship all at once; they moved it *plank by plank*. They *disassembled* the Spirit of Athens in Dock A and *reassembled* it in Dock B. The fact that they were also using the partially disassembled ship in dry-dock A as a kind of "blueprint" for building a new teak ship is simply irrelevant to *our* question. All we need to do is determine where Theseus's ship wound up at the *end* of the procedure—and there it is, every plank of it, in Dock B. How it *got* there—whether it was moved all at once or plank by plank—doesn't matter. All that's important is that it *did* get there. So it's Ship Y, the one in Dock B at the end of the procedure, that's Theseus's ship, the Spirit of Athens.

Now there are a number of interesting things to observe about these two answers. The first thing is that *both* of them are pretty "commonsensical." That's both a strength and a weakness. It's a strength in that it makes each answer *plausible*. Neither one is "wild" or "counterintuitive" or "off the wall," and apparently neither answer requires us to swallow any peculiar "metaphysical" principles about identity of the sort that academic philosophers are sometimes accused of advocating. The commonsensicality of both answers is a weakness, however, in that it makes each of them more or less *equally* plausible. While "common sense" may feel quite comfortable with *either* of these answers, in other words, it ought to begin to get a little nervous when it notices that it is no *more* comfortable with one of them than with the other. (This, by the way, is one good sign that you are dealing with a philosophical problem.) And so a second thing to notice is that these two answers bring us more or less to the *limits* of what "common sense" can do for us here. It will be necessary, in other words, to begin to do some detailed *philosophical* thinking about the problem. But what, exactly, does that mean?

Well, the third thing to notice about these two answers is that they are no longer *mere* opinions. They have become *reasoned* opinions. That is, each party to our little disagreement has not only expressed an opinion of what the correct answer *is*, but he or she has also offered an account of *why* we should accept the favored answer as the correct one. And that gives us something to *do* besides simply taking sides in the dispute. We can turn our attention from the original puzzle to an examination and evaluation of the *reasons* that have been offered in support of each suggested answer to the question.

It is important to realize that, when we do this, we will no longer be talking about which ship, X or Y, is the Spirit of Athens. As will shortly become clear, we will be talking about something else. We will, in fact, be talking about certain "common sense" views or convictions or, perhaps better, principles that each of our disputants is more or less *taking for granted* in reaching the conclusion that this or that ship, X or Y, is Theseus's ship, the Spirit of Athens. And so the next thing we need to do is to ask what each of our two disputants *is* taking for granted. What bits of common sense is each person *using* that he or she hasn't taken the trouble explicitly to *mention*? Let's see if we can, so to speak, tidy up the two lines of reasoning that have been offered and set them out in the form of an orderly, step-by-step argument, making explicit their premises and presuppositions.

The case for Ship X, we recall, focused on the fact that there was *some ship or other* parked in dry-dock A during the whole 1000t minutes. *Whenever* we took a "snapshot" of the shipyard, we would have found *a* (whole) ship sitting there. At minute 0, of course, the ship parked in Dock A is Theseus's ship, the Spirit of Athens. Now the case for Ship X grants that lots of things were *done to* the ship in Dock A during the ensuing 1000t minutes. But what it clearly takes for granted is that no one of the things which was done to it was sufficient to change its *identity*. And this, of course, was also what we were taking for granted in Story 2, when we concluded that the ship in Dock A at the end of the process, although made entirely of teak, was in fact the (fully renovated) ship with which we began, that is, the Maid of Thebes. In each case, our reasoning tacitly relies on repeated applications of something like the following principle: Replacing one part of a complex object does not affect the identity of that object. And that seems plausible. Changing the oil filter or spark plugs in your car does not result in your having a different car. It is surely this principle, repeatedly applied from minute to minute, that underlies the conviction that the ship originally parked in Dock A, whether it be the Maid of Thebes or the Spirit of Athens, *persists* in Dock A from minute to minute. Tidied up, then, the case for Ship X looks more or less like this:

Argument X:

1. The ship in Dock A at minute 0 is the Spirit of Athens.
2. Replacing one plank of a 1000-plank ship does not alter the identity of the ship.
3. The ship in Dock A at minute t differs from the ship in Dock A at minute 0 only in that one oak plank has been replaced by a teak plank.
4. So the ship in Dock A at minute t is the Spirit of Athens. [From 1, 2, 3]
5. The ship in Dock A at minute $2t$ differs from the ship in Dock A at minute t only in that one oak plank has been replaced by a teak plank.
6. So the ship in Dock A at minute $2t$ is the Spirit of Athens. [From 4, 2, 5]
7. But we can repeat this pattern of reasoning for minute $3t$, minute $4t$, minute $5t$, and so on, up to minute 1000t, each repetition reaching the intermediate conclusion that the ship in Dock A at that time is the Spirit of Athens.
8. So the ship in Dock A at minute 1000t is the Spirit of Athens.
9. But Ship X is the ship in Dock A at minute 1000t.
10. Hence, Ship X is Theseus's ship, the Spirit of Athens.

The case for Ship Y, on the other hand, focused on the fact that every *plank* in dry-dock B at minute 1000t started out at minute 0 in dry-dock A. What's more, the planks in Dock B at minute 1000t are interlocked together in exactly the same way in which they were interlocked together in Dock A at minute 0, when they indisputably constituted Theseus's ship, the Spirit of Athens. What this line of reasoning evidently takes for granted, then, is a principle that might be formulated as: A complex whole is *nothing but* the sum of its parts. And something like this, of course, was also what we were taking for granted in Story 1, when we concluded that the ship in Dock B at the end of the process was in fact the ship with which we began, that is, the Pride of Sparta. In each case, our reasoning tacitly relied on the conviction that if 1000 interlocked oak planks constitute a specific ship at minute 0, whether it be the Pride of Sparta or the Spirit of Athens, then, whatever may have happened to those planks during the intervening minutes, if they are later (at minute 1000t) again interlocked in exactly the same way as they were at minute 0, they will again constitute the *same* specific ship as they did at minute 0. Put in tidied-up form, then, the case for Ship Y looks something like this:

Argument Y:

1. A complex whole object (such as a ship) is nothing but the sum of its parts in a determinate arrangement.
2. The parts of Theseus's ship, the Spirit of Athens, are the 1000 sound and seaworthy oak planks of which it is composed at minute 0.
3. The parts of Ship Y are the 1000 sound and seaworthy oak planks of which *it* is composed at minute 1000t.
4. But every plank which is a part of Ship Y is (identical to) a plank which is a part of the Spirit of Athens.
5. Furthermore, the *arrangement* of the planks composing Ship Y is (plank-for-plank) identical to the arrangement of the planks composing the Spirit of Athens.
6. Hence, Ship Y *is* Theseus's ship, the Spirit of Athens. [From 1, 4, 5]

Like the two informal reasonings from which they are derived, each of our tidied-up arguments evidently leads to its desired conclusion. But, unlike the original informal reasonings, Arguments X and Y both make explicit certain general principles concerning parts and wholes and change which our hypothetical disputants were evidently taking for granted, principles which evidently played a crucial, if tacit, role in the reasonings which initially led to their differing conclusions. And now we are perfectly positioned to take the decisive step into *philosophical* reasoning. What we need to recognize is that, if our attempts to resolve the disagreement regarding which ship, X or Y, is the Spirit of Athens are to have *any* hope of succeeding, it is absolutely and crucially necessary for us to stop talking about the two *ships*, X and Y, and start talking about these two *arguments*, X and Y. The decisive step into philosophical reasoning, that is, consists precisely in *changing the subject!*

It does not help, in other words, for the advocate of Argument X (or Argument Y) simply to *reiterate* his or her argument for the favored conclusion, or even to produce *another*, different argument that leads to the same conclusion. Such measures may increase one party's *confidence* in the conclusion that he or she favors, but they take us no distance at all toward resolving the disagreement *between* our two advocates. Nor is anything gained when the advocate of Argument X (or Argument Y) simply insists that there must be *something* wrong with the opponent's reasoning. Of course, anyone who is committed to accepting the conclusion of one of these two arguments is *also* committed to believing that the conclusion of the other argument is false—and, *a fortiori*, if that other argument has a false conclusion, then there must be *something* wrong with it since a valid argument with true premises cannot lead to a false conclusion. But saying that there must be *something* wrong with the other argument is just more disagreeing; it is not making any progress toward *resolving* the disagreement.

For by saying only that there must be *something* wrong with an argument, you are not yet offering any *criticism* of it. You are only asserting your conviction that the argument in question is *susceptible* to criticism, that is, that it *can* be criticized, that it is criticiz*able*. And, of course, anyone who believes that the conclusion of some argument is false will also *believe* that the reasoning which leads to that false conclusion must itself be criticiz*able*. A wholly sound argument cannot possibly lead from true premises to a false conclusion.

Actually criticiz*ing* an argument, then, requires that you do more than disagree with its conclusion or insist that there must be *something* wrong with it. What you need to be able to do in addition is to give a specific diagnosis of *what* is wrong with it. And this implies that you will need to look *inside* the argument, not just at its conclusion. You will need to be able to find something *within* the argument of which you can say: "Here! *This* is the error. Just *here* is where the argument goes wrong, where my opponent's reasoning goes astray." And you will need to be able to back up these claims with *new* arguments—arguments not about Ship X and Ship Y or about the disputed conclusions, but rather about what you have identified as the trouble spot in you opponent's reasoning; arguments designed to show that what you are calling an error actually *is* an error.

Criticism must engage the argument. That is the decisive step into *philosophical* reasoning. The point is important enough to deserve being codified in the following way:

> Any opinion for which one can give reasons is admissible in philosophy, *but* once a claim has been supported by an argument, subsequent criticism *must* then engage the argument.

Rule One

In fact, the point is *so* important that there is no Rule Two.

What you need to know next, obviously, is *how* criticism can engage an argument. What is an argument, anyway, and what sorts of things can go wrong with one? These, consequently, will be the topics of my next chapters.

CHAPTER THREE

Engaging the Argument: Form

About the methods of philosophical inquiry little consensus can be achieved. But once we have separated, as best we can, issues of methodological substance from matters of philosophical style, it is likely that Rule One captures as much general agreement as we can hope for. The fundamental theme of Rule One is that philosophical views or positions require support by *argument*. By 'argument' I do not intend something essentially critical or contentious (although a philosopher can certainly be as negative and quarrelsome as anybody else). In its broadest sense, argument is simply the giving of reasons for beliefs. What Rule One insists is that although any view, however outrageous, may properly be introduced for philosophical discussion, its proponent is obligated to endeavor adequately to support that view by giving reasons for it, by producing arguments which subsequent critical exploration of the view can then usefully and fruitfully engage. This being so, we obviously need to take a closer look at arguments.

An argument may be thought of as a group or bunch or series of *statements*. In the cleanest sort of case, one of these statements will be tagged as the intended *conclusion*, expressing the target belief which requires support. Other statements will be marked as starting points or *premises*. The conclusion is what is argued *for*; the premises, what is argued *from*. The remaining statements will attempt to secure and illuminate a *connection* between the premises and the conclusion, to establish that one who grants the truth of the premises is thereby committed (or ought consistently to be committed) to granting as well the truth of the conclusion. There is thus an "iffy" claim that implicitly accompanies any argument: **If** one grants the truth of the premises, **then** one must (or should) grant the truth of the conclusion. The truth of the premises is to *guarantee* the truth of the conclusion. An argument for which this "iffy" claim is itself true is called a *valid* argument. Validity is thus an "iffy" property of arguments, a matter of the way in which the argument's premises and its conclusion are *related* to each other. Unlike truth and falsehood, validity is not a property of *individual* claims or statements. Nor, conversely, can an argument be true or false, although each of the individual statements composing it, including each of its premises and its conclusion, will presumably be either true or false.

Since the premises, the conclusion, and the intervening steps of an argument are all statements, in the ordinary way of statements they may individually be appraised as true or false. If the argument is a valid one, then from true premises it will arrive at a true conclusion. (That's what 'valid' *means*.) But now suppose that the conclusion reached in some argument is somehow undesirable. You don't like it. You disagree with it. You think that it's false, or even worse, that it's absurd. And so you would like to challenge it. How should you proceed?

Well, by now you should know that it won't do *simply* to disagree with the conclusion, to claim—or even to point out—that the conclusion is false or absurd. Philosophical criticism may begin with such disagreement, but it can't end there. However false or absurd the conclusion may be, there is still an argument to be dealt with. Philosophical criticism is *reasoned* criticism. In order to challenge the undesirable conclusion, in other words, it is necessary to challenge *directly* the course of reasoning which has been produced in support of it. Criticism must engage the argument. That's Rule One.

You may be firmly convinced that the argument isn't a good one. How could it be, if it leads to a false or absurd conclusion? But being convinced isn't enough. After all, the person who produced the argument in the first place is probably equally convinced that everything is quite in order. He may even grant that the conclusion *looks* false or paradoxical. "But," he is likely to go on, "the argument *commits us* to it." And if you continue, even quite properly, to insist that the conclusion is absurd, the most that its advocate is then required to concede is that the argument commits us to an absurd conclusion. But that does not change the fact that, as far as has yet been shown, the argument *does* commit us to it. In order to *escape* such a commitment, it is the argument itself, not just its conclusion, which must be called to account. It's not enough to believe that something has gone amiss. You need to find it. You need to show *what* is wrong with the argument. For the hard fact of the matter is this: If *nothing* can be shown to be wrong with the argument—if one cannot avoid accepting its premises and its reasoning—then one *is* committed to its conclusion, however false or absurd it may continue to seem. Rule One: Criticism must engage the argument. How, then, does one criticize an argument?

Well, what can go wrong with an argument? If the argument is a valid one, then from true premises it will arrive at a true conclusion. So if, in your judgment, a particular argument has arrived at a *false* conclusion, then one of two things must have happened: Either the argument *isn't* valid, or it *didn't* begin with true premises. This gives us two kinds of challenges to make. We can question the validity of the reasoning, or we can take issue with one or more of the premises. Both sorts of challenge deserve some detailed discussion.

Validity and Invalidity: Modeling Form

A challenge to a premise of an argument is a challenge to its *content*—to what it posits as *true*, the substantial theses from which it proceeds. In philosophy this sort of challenge presents special problems, special enough to deserve a chapter of their own. In due course, we shall come to them. But an argument is more than a mere collection or heap of statements. It is a group of statements that are intended to stand in supporting *relationships*. Recall the "iffy" claim which implicitly accompanies an argument: "**If** one grants the truth of the premises, **then** one must (or should) grant the truth of the conclusion." The conclusion, in other words, is supposed to *follow from* the premises. And this too is open to question.

You may, in other words, dispute an argument's implicit claim to validity. You can challenge, not the argument's content, but its *form*—and you can do this even if you accept all of the argument's premises. Whereas a critique of content addresses one or more of the premises individually with the challenge "That *isn't true*," a critique of form focuses instead on the *relation* between the conclusion and all the premises. Its challenge is: "That *doesn't follow*."

The general theoretical study of validity and invalidity, of what follows from what, is called *logic*. Because of the centrality of argument to philosophical practice, logic is one of the philosopher's most important conceptual tools. With the development of symbolic or mathematical logic in the twentieth century, logic has also emerged as an independent disciplinary specialty, on the boundary between philosophy and mathematics. (And, as you might guess, there is now also something called "the philosophy of logic.")

Although much of philosophical argumentation is too complex and elaborate to be reduced completely to symbolic or mathematical forms, there is no denying that the feedback from symbolic logic into traditional philosophical concerns has produced considerable clarification, purging philosophical reasoning of many invalid arguments which previously had been hardy perennials. It has been particularly helpful in sorting out the valid and invalid inferences which turn on the logical relationships of the *quantifiers*—'any,' 'every,' 'some,' and 'none'—and the *modalities*—'necessary,' 'possible,' and 'impossible' (about which more in the *next* chapter). In consequence, students who plan to pursue the study of philosophy with some seriousness beyond the introductory level are well advised to acquaint themselves with at least the rudiments of symbolic techniques. But since philosophers worked fruitfully with the concepts of validity and invalidity for hundreds of years before the development of these mathematical tools, there is obviously a good deal that one can accomplish without engaging in such specialized studies. Spelling out the implications of the "iffy" concept of validity will give us a better sense of what might be accomplished and of how to go about accomplishing it.

The critical fact about questions of validity and invalidity is that they are independent of an argument's *content*, that is, independent of the *topic* of the argument (what the argument is specifically *about*) and what its premises specifically *say* about that topic. Validity and invalidity are essentially matters of the *form* of arguments, that is, the *pattern* of relationships exhibited among various concepts, and so largely independent of what particular concepts actually enter into those patterned relationships. Just this is what makes it possible to treat logical notions mathematically. It is really only another way of stressing the "iffy" character of validity: "**If** the premises are true, **then** the conclusion must also be true." That is surely something that we ought to be able to know about an argument without knowing *whether* the premises or conclusion are true.

One's facility with the logical assessment of arguments can be improved, then, by developing an acquaintance with and sensitivity to recurring *patterns* of reasoning. Even a short time spent in the study of philosophy will suffice to equip you with a fairly sizable stock of elementary valid and invalid patterns on which to draw. But it would obviously be useful if we had, in addition, a *general* approach to assessing the validity or invalidity of some (perhaps unfamiliar) pattern of reasoning in a philosophical argument. A conclusive mechanical technique for testing arguments for validity or invalidity is, alas, not to be had, but we can at least sketch an informal *modus operandi* which, properly pursued, might occasionally save us from an undesirable conclusion by successfully challenging the validity of the reasoning that seems to lead to it.

What makes such a general approach possible is that *valid argument patterns necessarily lead from truths to truths.* This is just our "iffy" claim all over again: **If** the premises are true, **then** the conclusion must also be true. Conversely, if a pattern of reasoning *can* lead from truths to falsehoods, it cannot be a valid pattern. This observation gives us a handle on the problem of demonstrating invalidity. We can show that a given argument is invalid if we can find *another* argument which has the *same* pattern but which proceeds from obviously acceptable premises to an obviously unacceptable conclusion—that is, from premises whose truth is *not* in dispute to a conclusion whose falsehood is also *not* in dispute among the parties disagreeing about the original argument.

This is the technique of *modeling.* You extract, from the disputed original argument, the pattern of relationships that underlie the passage from its premises to its conclusion; and you then construct a second argument *on that model* which passes from undisputedly true premises to an undisputedly false conclusion. If you can do this, you will have established that the premises and conclusion of an argument *can* stand in that particular pattern of relationships even though the premises are true and the conclusion false. And *that*, in turn, implies that the particular pattern of relationships is *not* one for which the truth of the premises guarantees the truth of the conclusion. It follows that, even if the premises of the *original* argument are all true, the fact that they *do* stand in just that pattern of relationships to the original conclusion does *not*, by itself, commit one to accepting the truth of that conclusion.

Let's take a look at an example. Here are two short passages from René Descartes' first *Meditation:*

 I. Everything which I have thus far accepted as entirely true and assured has been acquired from the senses or by means of the senses. But I have learned by experience that these senses sometimes mislead me, and it is prudent never to trust wholly those things which have once deceived us.

 II. But perhaps God did not wish me to be deceived in that fashion, since he is said to be supremely good. But if it was repugnant to his goodness to have made me so that I was always mistaken, it would seem also to be inconsistent for him to permit me to be sometimes mistaken, and nevertheless I cannot doubt that he does permit it.[1]

We're not going to concern ourselves with the role of these passages in Descartes' larger project, or with the wide variety of philosophical queries which could be addressed to their sense or their presuppositions. What interests us here is

---

[1] René Descartes, *Meditations on First Philosophy,* trans. Laurence J. Lafleur (Indianapolis and New York: Bobbs-Merrill, 1960), pp. 18, 20.

only that each of these passages contains, or at least suggests, a little argument, and we are going to concern ourselves with these. In each of these passages, Descartes can be understood as proposing that something could always happen. In the first passage, for instance, he suggests that it could be the case that his senses always deceive or mislead him; in the second passage, that it could be the case that God always permits him to be mistaken. And in each instance, he gives a *reason* for supposing that what he is proposing is correct. In the first case, the reason is that his senses sometimes do mislead him; in the second, that God sometimes does permit him to be mistaken. Without too much violence, then, we can extract two tidied-up arguments from these two passages, each argument having one premise and a conclusion:

A1   My senses sometimes deceive me.
So, it could be the case that my senses always deceive me.

A2   God sometimes permits me to be mistaken.
So, it could be the case that God always permits me to
be mistaken.

Once we have come this far, a little reflection will suggest that we are dealing with two examples of a single *pattern* of reasoning, that our two arguments have a single *form*. One way of representing the common form of these two arguments is to retain the features which they share while replacing their specific differences in content by "dummies" or placeholders. If we do this with A1 and A2, making a few grammatical adjustments, what we get is this:

A*   X is sometimes F.
So, it could be the case that X is always F.

If we replace the letter 'X' by 'my senses' and the letter 'F' by 'deceptive' or 'misleading', we get argument A1. If we replace 'X' by 'God' and 'F' by 'willing to let me be mistaken', we get argument A2. We now have exactly the sort of representation of the *pattern* of relationships between the premise and the conclusion of both arguments that we need in order to apply the technique of modeling.

If we suspect that the argument form A* is in fact invalid, what we need to do, in order to *demonstrate* that it is, is to produce yet another argument of that *same* form with an undisputedly true premise and an undisputedly false conclusion. To put it differently, we need to find some other replacements for 'X' and 'F' in A* such that the sentence we get by replacing them in the premise is patently true and the sentence we get by making the same replacements in the conclusion is patently false. As it happens, this *is* an invalid argument form, and there are many possible pairs of expressions that we could make use of here. You may be able to think of some of your own, but here is one that occurred to me. Replace 'X' by 'paintings' and 'F' by 'forgeries'. What we then have, again tidying up the grammar, is the following argument:

A3   Paintings are sometimes forgeries
So, it could be the case that paintings are always forgeries.

The premise of A3 is obviously, as a matter of fact, true. But the conclusion of A3 is just as obviously false. A forged painting is a *copy* of some original painting, and it could not be the case that *all* paintings are copies. If no paintings were originals, there would be nothing for the supposed copies to be copies *of.* So the argument *pattern* A* is indeed an invalid pattern and, in consequence, both of the original arguments, A1 and A2, are invalid arguments. Neither argument establishes the truth of its conclusion.

It is important to appreciate exactly what we have just shown—and what we have *not* shown. In particular, we have *not* shown that the conclusions of A1 and A2 are false. We have shown only that, even if the premises of each argument are true, this fact does not by itself *guarantee* that the corresponding conclusions are also true. Validity, you should always remember, is an "iffy" property of arguments. So we haven't established that it couldn't always be the case that my senses are deceptive, and we haven't established that it couldn't always be the case that, despite his presumed perfect goodness, God permits me to be mistaken. To show either of those things would take yet another, still different, argument. What we *have* shown is that the fact that the sense are *sometimes* deceptive is not, by itself, a sufficient reason for believing that they could always be deceptive; and, similarly, the fact that God sometimes permits me to err would not, by itself, be a sufficient reason for believing that he could always permit it. We have shown, in other words, that the conclusions of A1 and A2 do not *follow* from the premises of those arguments, and thus that our accepting those premises as true does not *commit us* also to accept the conclusions as true. We may accept the premises and yet deny the conclusions without getting into any logical trouble. We have *not* determined whether Descartes' conclusions are right or wrong. What we have determined is that, even if he is right in both instances, he has not yet successfully *argued his case* in either. Consequently then, even if we should concede his premises we remain free to reject his conclusions. (Descartes, of course, is not finished. These were only tiny excerpts. He has lots of other arrows in his quiver.)

Princes and Frogs: Some Well-Known Patterns

Your skill in modeling argument forms will be facilitated, of course, if you have some idea of what you are looking for, some idea, that is, of what the form of an argument *might* be. It would be ideal if I could supply you with a checklist, so to speak—a complete enumeration of all the *possible* forms of argument, one of which would perforce have to be the form of the argument that you were interested in evaluating. Unfortunately, that is just impossible. There are an indefinite number of forms of argument, some of them incredibly complex and convoluted; and there is no way to predict in advance just what some philosopher will or will not come up with in an effort to establish his or her point.

What I *can* do, however, is provide a sampler of *some* useful and frequently used patterns of reasoning—patterns that also often appear as *pieces* of those larger and more intricate arguments that philosophers actually produce in support of their various claims. It will, in fact, be helpful to have examples of both valid and *in*valid forms of argument—both princes and frogs, as it were—since, alas, philosophers are simply not infallible logicians: one does occasionally find a froggy step in some philosopher's reasoning that has been happily masquerading as a princely valid argument.

In deductive reasoning, what characteristically gets the job done (or fails to do so) are certain "little words" (sometimes called *logical constants*) that signal logical relationships among the specific claims being made: 'if . . . then', 'not', 'either . . . or', 'both . . . and', 'all', 'every', 'some', 'none', and the like. You can often uncover a suitable "logical skeleton" by looking for the patterns that such little words create when you extract them from the specific topics being reasoned about. One way to organize an "argument sampler," then, is in terms of such little words, and that is the course I will follow here. To serve as premises and conclusions, I shall simply choose some dramatic, eye-catching "philosophical" claims. Since validity is an "iffy" property of arguments, for what we are up to here, it does not matter whether those premises and conclusions are *actually* true or false, although you will surely have opinions about some of them. Perhaps you will find yourself wondering just how you might go about evaluating and challenging not just the *form* of an argument but its *content* as well. That, of course, is a question which I've already postponed once, and the appropriate thing to do at this point is to postpone it again. We will turn to the matter of content in a subsequent chapter. For now, however, we have some forms to examine.

1.   **IF . . . THEN**

> **IF** abortion is murder, **THEN** abortion is morally wrong.
> Abortion *is* murder.
> So, abortion is morally wrong.

This princely valid argument form:

$$\frac{\textbf{IF } p \textbf{ THEN } q}{\text{So, } q} \quad p$$

is perhaps the simplest and most obvious traditional pattern of correct reasoning. It goes by the classical Latin name *modus ponens*. Notice that the second premise affirms the *antecedent* (the 'if'-part) of the 'if . . . then' *conditional*, first premise. The invalid froggy counterpart of this form, in contrast, affirms the conditional's *consequent* (the 'then'-part). "Affirming the consequent," in fact, is what it's called:

$$\frac{\textbf{IF } p \textbf{ THEN } q}{\text{So, } p} \quad q$$

For instance:

> **IF** the world was created by God, **THEN** it will exhibit order and lawfulness.
> The world *does* exhibit order and lawfulness.
> So, the world was created by God.

We can show the invalidity of this second form of argument easily enough by using the technique of modeling. Consider, for example, my dog Fido:

> **IF** Fido were a cat, **THEN** he'd have four legs and a tail.
> Fido *does* have four legs and a tail.
> _____
> So, Fido *is* a cat.

Both premises of this little model argument are plainly true. Its conclusion, however, is equally plainly false. The argument then is invalid (since, as you know, no *valid* argument can proceed from true premises to a false conclusion); and its *form,* "affirming the consequent," is indeed a genuine frog. (In most of the rest of this sampler, however, I shall generally leave it to you to find your own models to demonstrate the frogginess of the invalid forms of argument that I'll be exhibiting.)

2.   NOT with IF . . . THEN

Introducing a 'not' into our 'if . . . then' reasonings produces sort of a mirror image of the pure 'if . . . then' situation. Here, a princely argument looks like this:

> **IF** mental states are brain states, **THEN** they are located in space.
> But mental states are **NOT** located in space.
> _____
> So, mental states are **NOT** brain states.

In skeletal form, the valid pattern is:

> **IF** p **THEN** q
> **NOT** q
> _____
> So, **NOT** p

Notice that our second premise here denies the *consequent* (the 'then'-part) of the conditional first premise. If we instead deny the antecedent (the 'if'-part), what we obtain is an invalid froggy impostor that mimics our princely *modus ponens* arguments.

> **IF** God were at all evil, **THEN** the world could be better than it is.
> But God is **NOT** at all evil.
> _____
> So, the world could **NOT** be better than it is.

Or, in skeletal form:

> **IF** p **THEN** q
> **NOT** p
> _____
> So, **NOT** q

It is worth remarking that it's important, when constructing skeletons for the purposes of modeling, that each occurrence of a word, group of words, or sentence be replaced by the *same* "dummy" letter or placeholder every time it occurs. Conversely, when you are actually presenting a model argument, it is important that each place-holder in the skeleton be replaced by the *same* words or sentence every time that *it* occurs. Only in this way can you be sure that the model argument you end up with does indeed have the same form as the argument you originally set out critically to evaluate.

3.   BOTH . . . AND with NOT

The case of 'both . . . and' by itself, of course, is pretty straightforward. When 'and' is combined with 'not', however, we once again run the risk of confusing an invalid frog with a valid prince. Here, the princely argument looks like this:

> Space can**NOT** be **BOTH** finite and unbounded.
> Space *is* unbounded.
> ———————————————
> So, space is **NOT** finite.

(In case you're curious, by the way, the first premise of this argument happens to be false. I won't, however, venture to say anything about its conclusion.) When we skeletonize this valid argument, we get the form:

> **NOT BOTH** *p* **AND** *q*
>
> p
> ———————
> So, **NOT** *q*

Unfortunately, there is a frog in the vicinity.

> Mercy killing can**NOT** be **BOTH** morally obligatory **AND** morally wrong.
> It is surely **NOT** morally obligatory.
> ————————————————————
> So, mercy killing must be morally wrong.

Here, our skeleton is:

> **NOT BOTH** *p* **AND** *q*
> **NOT** *p*
> ———————
> So, *q*

And while this may look deceptively like our valid prince, a more careful scrutiny, accompanied by a little thought and a little modeling, should convince you that it is indeed a froggy impostor. (Consider, for example, that mercy killing might be *neither* morally obligatory *nor* morally wrong. It might, for instance, sometimes simply be morally *permitted*, without ever being an obligation or duty.)

4.   EITHER . . . OR with NOT

The case of 'or' is complicated by the fact we use the word both *exclusively* and *inclusively*. That is, sometimes '*p* or *q*' has the force of 'either *p* or *q*, but *not both*'—

for example, "I'll ask Abigail or Betty to the dance"; while at other times, it has the force of 'either *p* or *q* *or* both'—for example, "Feel free to take seconds of meat or potatoes." (This latter, inclusive sense is sometimes expressed in informal writing as "and/or".) Whether 'or' is being used exclusively or inclusively, however, if we can rule out one of the indicated alternatives, we can validly infer that the remaining alternative does hold. In other words, arguments of the form:

> **EITHER** *p* **OR** *q*
> **NOT** *p*
> ⎯⎯⎯⎯⎯
> So, *q*

are always valid. As an example, we can use:

> Values are **EITHER** discoverable properties of things (like colors) **OR** they are conventional products of arbitrary human decisions.
> But values are obviously **NOT** discoverable properties of things.
> ⎯⎯⎯⎯⎯⎯⎯⎯⎯⎯⎯⎯⎯⎯⎯⎯⎯⎯⎯⎯⎯⎯⎯⎯
> So, values must be conventional products of arbitrary human decisions.

Notice that this argument proceeds from the *falsity* of one alternative to the *truth* of the remaining alternative. We might also be tempted to suppose that it is equally in order to argue from the *truth* of one alternative to the *falsity* of the remaining alternative. That is, we might be tempted to accept the form:

> **EITHER** *p* **OR** *q*
> *p*
> ⎯⎯⎯⎯⎯
> So, **NOT** *q*

And it is true that *sometimes* reasoning in this way will not get us into any trouble. In particular, we know we are safe when our two alternatives, *p* and *q*, are logically *guaranteed* to be mutually exclusive—when, for instance, alternative *q* is simply the *negation* of alternative *p*, as in the example:

> Judith's argument is **EITHER** valid **OR** *in*valid.
> As we have seen, her argument is valid.
> ⎯⎯⎯⎯⎯⎯⎯⎯⎯⎯⎯⎯⎯⎯⎯⎯⎯⎯⎯⎯
> So, it is **NOT** *in*valid

As a special case, in other words, we can rely on the form:

> **EITHER** *p* **OR** *NOT-p*
> *p*
> ⎯⎯⎯⎯⎯⎯⎯
> So, **NOT** *NOT-p*

Nevertheless, we cannot in general accept the argument form in which the second premise affirms one of the two indicated alternatives as a true prince, for sometimes, alas, it *can* get us into trouble. That's why I earlier flagged it as a frog. Sometimes, that is, this form of reasoning *can* lead from true premises to a false conclusion. In fact, this can happen whenever 'or' is being used in the *inclusive* ("and/or") way, as, for instance, in the argument:

> Our tests show that **EITHER** your generator **OR** your distributor is defective.
> Now there's no doubt that your generator is defective.
> So, your distributor is **NOT** defective.

Here, of course, it could be the case that *both* the generator *and* the distributor are out of order. Only if we had an additional premise (say, reporting the results of further tests) which excluded this third possibility would we be entitled to conclude that the defective generator was the *whole* of the problem. Whenever it might be the case that 'or' is being used in this inclusive way, in other words, what we need to rule out one of the indicated alternatives is not an argument of the froggy form we've just been examining, but a more complicated argument—one of the form:

> **EITHER** p **OR** q
> **NOT BOTH** p **AND** q
> p
> So, **NOT** q

(If you're on your toes, you'll have noticed that, in *this* form of argument, the first 'either . . . or' premise is simply superfluous!) What happens in any *interesting* 'either . . . or' argument is, of course, that we cannot tell just by looking whether the 'or' is properly to be understood as inclusive ("and/or") or exclusive. Thus, for instance, in the argument:

> Sensations are **EITHER** mental **OR** physical.
> Sensations are obviously mental.
> So, sensations are **NOT** physical.

it is not clear that we can, without further argument, rule out the possibility that sensations are *both* mental *and* physical; and *since* we have not ruled out that possibility, the argument as it stands is invalid.

5.   EVERY . . . and SOME

When they appear in premises or conclusions by themselves, 'every' and 'some' tend to be well behaved. It is primarily when we combine them in a single claim about the relationships between two groups of items that we find an occasional frog peeking out at us from among the princes. As it happens, it is easiest to illustrate points about 'every' and 'some' with familiar *mathematical* examples, so let us take our two groups of items to be the positive integers (1,2,3,4, . . .) and the integers in general (including zero and the negative integers). Since −1 is smaller than every positive integer, the following princely argument is not only valid, but also sound. That is, it has a true premise and so, also, a true conclusion as well.

> There is **SOME** integer that is smaller than **EVERY** positive integer.
> So, for **EVERY** positive integer, there is **SOME** integer smaller than it.

Now it may seem as if we are simply *repeating* ourselves when we offer the conclusion of this argument as something that follows from its premise—but therein lies the froggy peril. For consider the following argument:

> For **EVERY** integer, there is **SOME** positive integer larger than it.
> So, there is **SOME** positive integer that is larger than **EVERY** integer.

Once again we begin with a true premise, but here, of course, the conclusion does not "follow" at all! On the contrary, it explicitly contradicts something that we know independently to be true, namely that there is no *largest* integer (for we can always add 1 to any integer and thereby produce a larger one). It is crucially important, in short, to get our 'every' and our 'some' in such claims in the correct *order*. Whereas arguments of the form:

> There is **SOME** x that is *R*-related to **EVERY** y.
> So, for **EVERY** y, there is **SOME** x that is *R*-related to it.

are valid, in other words, arguments of the form:

> For **EVERY** x, there is **SOME** y that is R-related to it.
> So, there is **SOME** y that is R-related to **EVERY** x.

are *not*. Just remind yourself that, although it's true that

> For **EVERY** son, there is **SOME** woman who is his mother.

it's plainly false that

> There is **SOME** woman who is the mother of **EVERY** son.

and you will never go astray!

Three More Useful Patterns

Since the set of possible forms of argument is literally inexhaustible, any decision to break off a collection of examples at this or that point must, in the end, be a matter of judgment. We soon find ourselves wishing for some *general* tools for handling *all sorts* of arguments—and that, indeed, is just what is provided by the discipline of formal (mathematical or symbolic) logic. To undertake the presentation of a mini-course in formal logic *here*, however, would unfortunately be a clear example of very poor judgment. The topic is simply too complex to be usefully treated with such brevity. Nevertheless, good judgment dictates, I think, that I not abandon the theme of argument forms without at least mentioning three more valid patterns of reasoning that often prove to be especially useful—so useful, in fact, that they tend to show up very frequently whenever philosophers (and even non-philosophers) set out to attempt to establish a conclusion.

The first of these patterns is characteristically found in so-called "case studies"—arguments in which a complex situation is broken down into a series of alternative *possibilities*. If *each* alternative can then separately be shown to imply a certain conclusion, then although we may not be able to determine which of the various possibilities is *in fact* the case, we can nevertheless validly infer that this conclusion is itself true. When there are just two possibilities, *p* and *q*, for example, the pattern looks like this:

> **EITHER** *p* **OR** *q*
> **IF** *p* **THEN** *r*
> **IF** *q* **THEN** *r*
> _____
> So, *r*

Here's an example:

> Human actions are **EITHER** causally determined **OR** mere random occurrences.
> **IF** human actions are determined by external causes, **THEN** they do not arise from our exercise of free will
> But **IF** human actions are mere random events, **THEN** once again we do not exercise free will.
> _____
> So, there is no free will

When the outcome of such reasoning is uncomfortable (as it is, perhaps, in this example), the argument is often called a *dilemma*. The two alternative possibilities mentioned in the 'either . . . or' premise are then called the *horns* of the dilemma. When someone's argument threatens to "impale you on the horns of a dilemma," there are three things you can do in order to escape.

1. You can challenge the *first* 'if . . . then' premise by granting the first alternative, *p*, while arguing that it does *not* lead to the uncomfortable result, *r*. This is called "swallowing the first horn of the dilemma."
2. Similarly, you can challenge the *second* 'if . . . then' premise by granting the second alternative, *q*, while arguing that *it* does not lead to the uncomfortable result, *r*. This is called "swallowing the second horn of the dilemma."
3. Or, finally, you can challenge the 'either . . . or' premise by arguing that the two *enumerated* alternatives, *p* and *q*, do not exhaust *all* of the possibilities, that is, that something has been overlooked. And this is called "trying to run *between* the horns of the dilemma."

The remaining two useful argument patterns both establish their conclusions by reasoning from *hypotheses*. In these cases, one of the premises is not *asserted* as something which the arguer is committed to accepting as true, but rather merely temporarily *supposed*, "for the sake of argument," to see what conclusions one could derive from it *if* it were true. As you might expect, then, this is the pattern of reasoning generally employed when someone is interested in establishing a *conditional* conclusion, one which is itself "iffy". In such a case, the argument skeleton looks something like this:

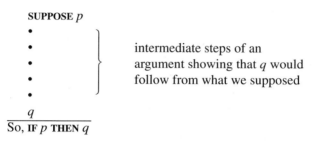

Here's a potentially poignant example (where, you will notice, some of the intermediate steps happen to have the form of a dilemma):

> SUPPOSE that there exists some being (call him "Otto") who is omniscient.
> Now, it's either true that I will go swimming next Tuesday, or it's true that I will *not* go swimming next Tuesday.
> If it's true that I will go swimming next Tuesday, then (since an omniscient being knows all truths), Otto now *knows* that I will.
> And, if it's true that I *won't* go swimming next Tuesday, then Otto now knows that I won't.
> So, in either case, Otto now knows what I will do next Tuesday.
> But the same line of reasoning can be applied to *any* of my future actions and, indeed, to any of *anyone's* future actions.
> So Otto now knows what *all* of *everyone's* future actions will be.
> But then all of our future actions must be *already determined*, and I am not genuinely free to *choose*, for example, whether or not to go swimming next Tuesday.
> However, free will requires the ability to make genuine choices.
> Hence, no-one has free will.
> So, IF there exists an omniscient being, THEN no-one has free will.

The second, even more common application of such hypothetical reasoning is its use to show that some claim is *false*, by arguing that, if we supposed otherwise (that is, if we supposed that the claim was *true*), disastrous consequences would ensue. In this instance, of course, the "disastrous consequences" are only *logically* disastrous. In particular, they consist in the derivation of some *absurdity*, either the derivation of a straightforward self-contradiction (often including the negation of the very claim we began by supposing) or, less dramatically, the derivation of some further claim that all parties to the discussion *agree* is simply obviously false. This form of argument, in fact, is traditionally called *reductio ad absurdum* ("reduction to an absurdity"). In skeletal form, such arguments look like this:

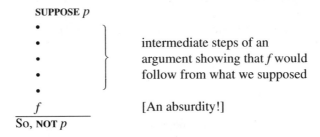

SUPPOSE *p*

intermediate steps of an
argument showing that *f* would
follow from what we supposed

f   [An absurdity!]
_____
So, **NOT** *p*

For our last example, let us travel to the wonderful island of the knights and the knaves, explored along with other strange territories in charming detail by Raymond Smullyan in his delightful book, *What Is the Name of This Book?—The Riddle of Dracula and Other Logical Puzzles* (Prentice-Hall, Inc.: Englewood Cliffs, N.J., 1978). What you need to know about the inhabitants of this island is that knights *always* tell the truth, whereas knaves *always* lie. Thus, when you come across two natives, Ambrose and Boris, if Ambrose should happen to remark "At least one of us is a knave," you could correctly reason:

> **SUPPOSE** that Ambrose is a knave.
> Then, since knaves always lie, what Ambrose said must be false.
> That is, it is false that at least one of them is a knave.
> But then both of them, including Ambrose, must be knights.
> That is, Ambrose must be both a knave (for that's what we're supposing) *and* a knight (for that's what the supposition implies). [An absurdity!]
> _____
> So, Ambrose is **NOT** a knave.

(And, parenthetically, you could now also go on to conclude that Boris *is* a knave, since Ambrose, whom you now know to be a knight, has said that at least one of them is a knave, and knights *always* tell the truth.)

Dilemma, argument from hypothesis, and *reductio ad absurdum*—three useful patterns. But there is much more to the notion of an argument's *form* than what can be, as it were, read off from the patterns of logical constants explicitly occurring in its premises and conclusion. I would be remiss to leave the topic, I think, without first trying to convey to you some sense of the *subtleties* on which criticisms that appeal to the notion of form can rest—and then giving you a few more tools for dealing with them, too.

Minding One's Modifiers:
Form with Finesse

There are a number of important patterns of reasoning we've not yet examined which turn crucially on *modifiers*, words which make their contribution to what is being said by attaching themselves to other words to form complex expressions whose implications and other logical relationships are often changed in surprising and unexpected ways. Simply *relocating* a modifier within the structure of a sentence can frequently lead to quite dramatic alterations in what one can properly infer from what is being said, as can different interpretations of *how much* of a whole sentence a given modifier is intended to apply to. What it's appropriate to treat as the *logical* form of premises or conclusions, in other words, unfortunately does not always track tidily with the superficial *grammatical* forms of the idioms used to express them. The easiest way to see this is by learning about hidden 'if's.

Hidden 'If's

It is wartime. Deep in occupied territory, a small group of resistance fighters finds their plans repeatedly thwarted. Someone must be informing the enemy. There is a traitor in their midst. Their leader lays a careful trap—and it succeeds! It turns out that *two* enemy agents have infiltrated the group. Nigel and Elena have both been passing on information about the partisans' plans. What should be done about them? Reluctantly the group's leader pronounces the difficult verdict:

(S1)   The traitors will be shot.

Only this last remark concerns us here. Suppose we regard (S1) as a *premise*. What does it imply? That is, what can we legitimately conclude from it? Well, at least on the face of it, we are surely entitled to at least this much:

(S)   *Someone* will be shot.

Indeed, we might add, in the context of our little drama, the leader could evidently just as well have said

(S1´)   Nigel and Elena will be shot,

and there's no doubt that *this* implies that someone will be shot.

But let's change the scene. In this new story let us suppose I am on an enjoyable cross-country walking tour of the British Cotswolds when I find my way blocked by a low stone wall. Just as I'm about to climb over it and continue along in the direction I've been going, I notice a sign nailed to a nearby tree:

(S2)   Trespassers will be shot.

Taking the sign seriously, I prudently decide to head back to where I came from.

On first encounter, (S2) may well appear to have the same form as (S1). But does (S2) also imply (S), that someone will be shot? Obviously it does not. Unlike (S1), (S2) can be true even though no one is ever shot, for it might be the case that no one ever trespasses. In the present story, for instance, *I* didn't trespass, and the *reason* I didn't do so was precisely my belief that what the sign said was true. But, if the sign doesn't say anything that implies that someone will be shot, then just what *does* it say? Well, just what did I *believe* that effectively changed my mind about which way to go? Surely it must have been something like this: that *if* I trespassed, *then* I might well be shot. The most useful way to understand (S2), in other words, is to see it as containing a hidden 'if':

(S2´)   *If* anyone trespasses, *then* he or she will be shot.

Such a hidden 'if' also explains, for instance, how it can be true that

(H1)   Unicorns have exactly one horn,

despite the fact that there are no unicorns.[1] That is, (H1) is best interpreted on the model of (S2´), as:

(H1´)   IF anything is a unicorn, THEN it has exactly one horn.

(And, parenthetically, there is more than one way to hide an 'if.' Here, for instance, we could also say, "Nothing is a unicorn *unless* it has exactly one horn.") In short, sentence (H1) says something about one of the conditions an animal satisfies *if*, so to speak, it qualifies as a unicorn; but (H1) does not say whether or not anything *does* qualify as a unicorn. Similarly,

(H2)   Cows have exactly two horns,

tells us one of the conditions an animal satisfies *if* it qualifies as a cow. Of course, we

---

[1] If you happen to believe that there *are* unicorns, you can substitute the example "Griffins have hooked beaks." If you happen *also* to believe that there are griffins, however, you should seriously consider temporarily abandoning the study of philosophy in favor of some remedial mythology and zoology.

happen to know that something *does* qualify as a cow—but (H2) doesn't tell us that. Like (S2) and (H1), (H2) is best interpreted as making only a *conditional* claim, that

(H2′)   IF anything is a cow, THEN it has exactly two horns.

Then, if we want to convey the *additional* information that, indeed, something *does* qualify as a cow, nothing prevents us from adding a further conjunct which explicitly says so:

(H2e)   IF anything is a cow, THEN it has exactly two horns, AND there are cows.[2]

As you might expect, such hidden 'if's can be confusing in their own right. But they become especially dangerous when they are combined with those slippery modalities.

Those Slippery Modalities

Some statements are not merely true, but appear to be *necessarily* true: for example, "Every triangle has exactly three sides." That not only *is* true, we might say, it *must* be true. Similarly, other statements are apparently not only false, but also *necessarily* false; For example, "Some odd numbers are evenly divisible by two." That *couldn't be* true. Alternatively we might say that it's *impossible* for an odd number to be evenly divisible by two. And yet other statements, we're inclined to say, are neither necessarily true nor necessarily false. They're true or false simply as a matter of fact, *contingently* true or false. "The author of this book has a daughter," for instance, is contingently true. "The author of this book is a bachelor" is contingently false. In this case, although in fact I *do* have a daughter, it *could* have been true that I didn't; and similarly, although I am actually *not* a bachelor, it *could* have been true that I was. The contrary of any matter of fact, as the philosopher David Hume once said, is always *possible*. Necessity, possibility, and impossibility are collectively known as *modalities*—and the modalities are a slippery bunch. Their territory simply teems with frogs.

Two related phenomena account for much of this frogginess. One is that the modalities are most naturally informally indicated either by *auxiliary verbs* (the so-called "modal auxiliaries")—characteristically by various inflections of 'must' and 'can' (including 'could' and 'couldn't')—or by *modal adverbs* such as 'necessarily'

---

[2]   And having come this far, it is worth noting that we can extend this treatment to our earlier example, (S1), "The traitors will be shot," interpreting it as:

(S1e)   If anyone is a traitor, then he or she will be shot, and there are some traitors.

And since we're now regarding "Traitors will be shot" as saying only that someone will be shot *if* he or she is a traitor, we here begin to see what sort of *logical* work gets done by the little definite article, 'the'.

and 'possibly.' Auxiliary verbs, as their description indicates, are "helper" verbs; like adverbs, they modify *other* verbs (including, of course, the verb "to be"). In connection with sentences that contain only one main verb, this fact generally causes no trouble. But many sentences have *several* main verbs, and in that case it becomes crucially important to figure out the precise *scope* of the indicated modality, that is, whether it is intended to apply to the *whole* sentence or only to the *part* of the sentence whose main verb is (from the grammatical point of view) getting modified. In particular, "iffy" sentences have two main verbs; and, quite independently of the intended scope of the modality, correct idiomatic usage characteristically attaches a modal modifier to the verb appearing in the sentence's 'then' part:

(M1)   If Chuck is an uncle, then he CAN'T be an only child.

(M2)   If Carol is an aunt, then she NECESSARILY has a niece or a nephew.

Whether someone is an only child or has a niece or a nephew, of course, is always a matter of fact. That Chuck is (or isn't) an only child or that Carol does (or doesn't) have a niece or nephew is only *contingently* true or false. Although the modal modifier is grammatically attached to the verb in the *consequent* of each conditional sentence, then, it's only what is indicated by the *whole* 'if ... then' sentence that can correctly be described as impossible or necessary:

(M1*)   It CAN'T be true that [Chuck is *both* an uncle *and* an only child].

(M2*)   It's NECESSARILY true that [*if* Carol is an aunt *then* she has a niece or a nephew].

The second frog-generating fact about the modalities is that modal adverbs and auxiliaries are also informally and idiomatically used *contextually* in a *conclusion* as a kind of emphatic comment on the cogency of the argument leading up to it:

(AM-1)   Richard was stabbed in San Jose on the 15th.
          Jack was in Singapore from the 12 to the 18th.
          So, it is IMPOSSIBLE for Jack to have stabbed Richard.

(AM-2)   Every psychiatrist has attended medical school.
          Sue is a psychiatrist.
          So, Sue MUST have attended medical school.

Each of *these* modal indicators is simply a way of stressing the *validity* of the corresponding *non*-modal reasoning:

(A-1)   Richard was stabbed in San Jose on the 15th.
         Jack was in Singapore from the 12 to the 18th.
         So, Jack didn't stab Richard.

(A-2)   Every psychiatrist has attended medical school.
                  <u>Sue is a phychiatrist.</u>
            So, Sue attended medical school.

What is impossible, in other words, is not that Jack stabbed Richard (period). Whether or not one person did or didn't stab another is always a matter of fact. What *is* impossible is that both premises of the valid argument (A-1) are true and its conclusion—that Jack didn't stab Richard—is nevertheless false. That is, *given* that the premises of (A-1) are true, it *follows* that Jack didn't stab Richard. Similarly, what *must* be the case is not that Sue attended medical school (period). That someone does or doesn't attend medical school is always only contingently true or false. What *must* be the case is rather that *if* the premises of the valid argument (A-2) are true, then so is its conclusion, that Sue attended medical school. *Given* that both premises of (A-2) are true, it *follows* that Sue attended medical school.

Now, in light of these observations, think for a moment about the following pattern of reasoning:

(AMC)   *F*'s are NECESSARILY *G*.
                  <u>*x* is an *F*</u>
            So, *x* MUST be *G*

A little reflection will make it clear that (AMC) can be the skeleton of *four* different argument forms. The *first* thing we need to attend to, of course, is the fact that the first premise here is best interpreted as containing one of those hidden 'if's. Making this explicit, we would arrive at the argument skeleton:

(AMC*)   IF something is an *F*, THEN it is NECESSARILY *G*.
                  <u>*x* is an *F*</u>
            So, *x* MUST be *G*

There remain, however, the two modal expressions to be dealt with, the 'necessarily' in the conditional first premise and the 'must' in the conclusion.

On the one hand, the intended *scope* of the modality in the first premise can be either the whole 'if . . . then' conditional or just its consequent (the 'then' part). We can explicitly indicate this difference by contrasting

It's NECESSARILY TRUE that [IF something is an *F*, THEN it's also *G*].

with   IF something is an *F*, THEN it's NECESSARILY TRUE that [it's also *G*].

The square brackets signal the intended scope of the modality. On the other hand, the modal auxiliary occurring in the *conclusion* sentence can either be intended to indicate that it is supposed to express a necessary truth or be understood as merely making one of those contextual comments on the validity of the argument as a whole. We can indicate this difference by contrasting

It's **NECESSARILY TRUE** that [*x* is *G*]

with   *IT FOLLOWS THAT: x* is *G*.

And when we take apart (AMC) using these tools, what we find are three princely argument forms but also, alas, one nasty frog. Here, first, are the princes:

IF something is an *F,* **THEN** it is **NECESSARILY TRUE** that [it's also *G*].

x is an *F*

So, it's **NECESSARILY TRUE** that [*x* is *G*].

IF something is an *F,* **THEN** it is **NECESSARILY TRUE** that [it's also *G*].

x is an *F*

So, *IT FOLLOWS THAT: x* is *G*.

It's **NECESSARILY TRUE** that [**IF** something is an *F,* **THEN** it's also *G*].

x is an *F*

So, *IT FOLLOWS THAT: x* is *G*.

And here is the frog:

It's **NECESSARILY TRUE** that [**IF** something is an *F,* **THEN** it's also *G*].

x is an *F*.

So, it's **NECESSARILY TRUE** that [*x* is *G*].

The handiest tool for coping with the modalities comes from the work of the great German philosopher and mathematician G.W. Leibniz. Leibniz's ingenious suggestion was that there is a way of pairing up modal arguments with arguments whose validity or invalidity turns only on the so-called *quantifiers*, that is, such notions as 'every', 'some', and 'none'. What Leibniz proposed was that we think of our world, the *actual* world, as just one of countless *possible* worlds. We can then replace each *modal* statement with a corresponding statement about the truth of its *non-modal core*—the sentence to which the modal modifier applies—in various possible worlds. On this interpretation, a statement will, for instance, be *necessarily* true just in case it is true in *all* possible worlds. Similarly, to say that a statement expresses a *possibility* (is *possibly* true) will be to make the more limited claim that it is true in *some* possible world, and a sentence will be used to say something *impossible* just in case what it says is true in *no* possible world.

Leibniz's strategy is especially useful for sorting out *mixed* arguments whose validity or invalidity turns on both modalities and quantifiers. Consider, for example, a modification of the little argument regarding sensory experience that we earlier extracted from some passages by Descartes:

B   *Any* sensory experience *could* be deceptive.
So, it *could* be the case that *all* sensory experiences are.

Is this a valid argument, or is it invalid? Well, what shall we take as the argument's form? How should we tidy it up?

The premise of argument B says something modal about sensory experiences *considered one at a time* (i.e., considered *severally*, as we sometimes say). We can understand it along the following lines: Pick an experience. Then it is *always* true of the individual experience you've picked that *it* could be deceptive. The conclusion, in contrast, says something modal about sensory experiences *considered all together* (i.e., considered *collectively*), namely that it could be the case that there are no *non*-deceptive experiences, that *every* sensory experience is deceptive. Following these leads suggests something along the lines of

B′   For EVERY sensory experience, it's POSSIBLE that it is deceptive.
So, it's POSSIBLE that EVERY sensory experience is deceptive.

That gives us an argument skeleton all right:

For EVERY *F*, it's POSSIBLE that it is *G*.
So, it's POSSIBLE that EVERY *F* is *G*.

But is it a prince or a frog?

Let's try Leibniz's strategy. In place of "it's possible," let us insert "it's true in some possible world." Our argument skeleton will then look like this:

For EVERY *F*, it's true in SOME possible world that it is *G*.
So, it's true in SOME possible world that EVERY *F* is *G*.

And I'll just bet you can now figure out what to say about these patterns of reasoning. Just think about it. Your mother would be proud of you!

Why Location Counts

I introduced the notion of *scope* in connection with modalities and conditional or 'if . . . then' sentences, but the question of what a given modifier is supposed to be modifying is one that it is generally worthwhile to keep in mind. Just as it's a good idea to ask yourself precisely what is supposed to be necessary or possible whenever you encounter a 'necessarily' or a 'possibly', so too, when you meet a 'clearly' or an 'obviously', it's an equally good idea to ask yourself just what is supposed to be clear or obvious. The answer to *that* question is not always clear or obvious.

What can well make the crucial difference or give you an essential clue is the *placement* of a modifier within a sentence. Location counts. It counts a lot. I shall consequently take my leave of this chapter and the topic of form with what I hope will be a memorable illustration of just how much it counts. You may be surprised. For this trick, I will need one *very* simple sentence:

(C)   I eat cookies,

and one modifier, an old friend, namely, '*only*'. There are exactly three places in this sentence where we can insert this modifier—but look at what comes out:

(C1)   Only I eat cookies.

Only *I* eat cookies. *He* doesn't eat them. *She* doesn't eat them. And you don't get any either!

(C2)   I only eat cookies.

I only *eat* cookies. I don't *bake* them. I don't *sell* them. I don't even *crumble* them.

(C3)   I eat only cookies.

I eat only *cookies*. At every meal. Cookies, cookies, cookies. It's an incredibly monotonous diet.

So location really does count—a lot! And, by the way, take a look at some of *your own* 'only's. Have you parked them in the right places? You may be surprised.

Hidden 'if's, slippery 'must's and 'can's, and floating 'only's—matters of form can be very subtle indeed. But, as we have already several times remarked, there is more to any argument than just its form. Every argument also has a *content*, a distinctive set of premises and presuppositions that are themselves being put forward by the argument's author as *truths*. When an argument is formally impeccable but, for all that, still results in a conclusion that you judge to be false, then it is necessary to come to terms with its content, to issue a challenge directly to one of those premises or presuppositions. How one goes about *doing* that is finally, as long promised, the topic of the next chapter.

CHAPTER FIVE

Engaging the Argument: Content

Challenging Premises: Beyond Mere Disagreement

A reasonably judicious and experienced philosopher is not likely to be found advancing straightforwardly invalid arguments. (Indeed, when a well-known philosopher did so a number of years ago, the case became a matter of some notoriety—"X's Logical Lapse," it was called—and the journals were temporarily filled with articles by colleagues trying to figure out what the fellow could possibly have had in mind.) Usually, that is, the *form* of the argument, the pattern of reasoning, will itself be in order. If the argumentation leads to an uncomfortable or unacceptable conclusion, then, it will be necessary to engage not the form but the *content*. You will, in short, need to go after one or more of the argument's premises, that is, to challenge the truth of the philosopher's starting points.

As in the case of conclusions, however, mere disagreement with a premise is not enough. Like the mere denial of a conclusion, the mere denial of a premise indicates no more than a difference of opinion. That is, it is never sufficient just to *say* that some premise is false and should be abandoned. It is always necessary to *show* that it is. But how does one do that?

Philosophy, you will recall, is a "second-order" discipline. The practicing philosopher characteristically operates at one remove from the "first-order" facts and normally lacks the sort of first-order *expertise* that would be needed in order to exhibit the falsehood of a premise by direct recourse to, for instance, data or experiments. Nor is the other philosopher, the one with whom he or she disagrees, likely to be any better off in this respect. Disagreements about the truth of premises, in other words, are typically *not* addressed by one or both of the disputing parties abandoning the role of a practicing philosopher in favor of, for instance, the role of a practicing natural or behavioral scientist. But then, under these circumstances, what sort of challenge *can* be mounted against a premise?

Well, what needs to be done is to provide the *advocate* of the disputed premise —that is, the philosopher who originally offered the argument that made use of it— some *reason* for abandoning it. Here again, philosophical criticism remains reasoned disagreement. But, given the "second-order" character of philosophy, how is one to accomplish this? There is one primary technique—and if you properly appreciate it, you will be on the high road to grasping everything that's special about the practice of philosophy. The technique is to provide an *internal* criticism. You meet your philosophical opponent, not in the archives or in the laboratory, but on his or her home court. You try to show that the premise in question is one which that philosopher cannot *consistently* believe to be true. That is, you try to show that, in the context of other *accepted* beliefs, the philosopher's regarding that premise as true lands him or her in trouble. It commits the philosopher to accepting something else that he or she doesn't *want* to accept—ideally, something that he or she has already explicitly denied, but in any case something that must consistently be rejected. (There are, in fact, various ways that a philosopher can "land in trouble." Later we will have occasion to take a detailed look at a number of them, but for now I shall limit my discussion to one central case.)

The *way* in which you do this, not surprisingly, is by constructing an argument of your own—ideally, an argument whose premises are a bunch of views, theses, claims, or positions *all* of which (including, of course, the disputed premise) are *accepted* by the philosopher whose argument you are challenging, but whose conclusion is a thesis that he clearly and explicitly *rejects*.

I want to go over this business very slowly and carefully, for if you grasp it you will have overcome what is probably the major obstacle to understanding how philosophers operate. So suppose that philosopher 1 offers an argument that proceeds from some premises—say, A, B, and C—to a conclusion, T, which philosopher 2 believes to be mistaken:

Philosopher 1:	A
(1st argument)	B
	C
	So, T

Since philosopher 2 is convinced that T is false, there is a disagreement—and wherever there is philosophical disagreement, Rule One applies! Philosopher 2 must now challenge the *argument* that has been offered by philosopher 1. Otherwise there is *merely* a disagreement, but no evident possibility of progress. That argument, let us suppose, is formally in good order. So 2 focuses on one of 1's *premises*; she believes, say, that premise A is false. In other words, she concludes that the way philosopher 1, although reasoning validly, was nevertheless able to reach a false conclusion, namely T, was by including in his argument a false premise, namely A.

On the other hand, philosopher 1, since he did take it as a premise, evidently believes that A is true. So the disagreement has now spread; it has been transferred from T to A. But the object of the game is to get beyond *mere* disagreement. What philosopher 2 must now do is attempt to supply 1 with some reason for *giving up* A. In the most straightforward case, what she does is this: Philosopher 1 will be explicitly on record as accepting, in addition to A, B, C, and T, various other theses—say U, V, and W; and as rejecting still others—say, X, Y, and Z. Philosopher 2 tries to select from the collection of additional theses that 1 *accepts* (U, V, W) a group which, when combined with A, will imply the truth of one of the theses that he *rejects*, such as X. In other words, she constructs an *argument* which proceeds from the premises U, V, . . . , A to the conclusion X.

Philosopher 2:	U
(2nd argument,	V
abbreviated)	•
	•
	•
	A
	So, X

And, if *this* argument is a good one, philosopher 1 is stuck. He must give up *something*. Philosopher 2, of course, promptly suggests that A is what must go, thereby undermining 1's original case for T—which, you will recall, is where all this started.

But philosopher 1 has a *variety* of options at this point. He may, for instance, indeed give up A—but then go on to offer *another* argument for the disputed original thesis T. Or he may hang on to A and abandon U, V, or W instead. Or he can change his mind about X, and make appropriate modifications in his other views. And there is still another possibility—traditionally the most disheartening one for a student to contemplate: 1 may criticize the new argument that has just been offered by 2.

For, of course, things are never really as tidy as I've made them out to be. In the usual case, 2 won't have been able to construct her rebuttal argument using *only* premises U, V, . . . , A that 1 is explicitly on record as accepting. Typically, 2 will have made use of some additional, auxiliary premises—say, D, E, and F—about which 1 has so far expressed no opinions:

Philosopher 2:	U
(2nd argument,	V
in full)	D
	E
	F
	A
	So, X

and philosopher 1 may decide to take issue with one of *those* premises. And, of course, to do that, he will need to construct *yet another* argument—for Rule One still applies!—and so it goes.

Several important points emerge from an examination of this pattern of challenge and response:

1. The original disagreement between philosophers 1 and 2 is over the truth or falsehood of some conclusion T which perhaps expresses an important and major thesis. But Rule One's requirement that criticism engage the arguments quickly causes T to drop out as a *visible* theme of the ongoing discussion. The actual battles will be fought at some remove from T—for instance, over A and E.

2. Furthermore, as the discussion develops, it rapidly emerges that the actual clash operates not simply over the isolated thesis T, but between two whole *systematic structures* of beliefs within which T or its denial is embedded. For a dispute of this sort comes to an end only when one of the disputants cannot, by appropriate challenges and adjustments, get his or her *whole* position—*all* the claims that he or she is committed to accepting or rejecting—to hang together coherently.

3. But the most important observation is this: The discussion always proceeds by answering argument with argument. And from the very first step, what the challenge arguments are *about* is always some aspect—the form or the content—of *another* argument.

Observation 1 accounts for the apparent *triviality* of some philosophical disputes. Beginning students in philosophy frequently complain that philosophers waste their time discussing inconsequential puzzles rather than important issues. Instead of directly facing the question "Is there an immortal soul?" they debate the question "Can I consistently imagine myself witnessing my own funeral?" Instead of taking on "What are the limits of perceptual knowledge?" they discuss "Can I tell whether I'm awake or dreaming?" Instead of offering an answer to "Are a person's acts free or determined?" philosophers consider "Does 'He could have done otherwise' imply 'He would have done otherwise if he had chosen'?" And so on.

Frustrating as all this frequently is to a beginning student, we can now see it as a consequence of the character of philosophical problems and philosophical method. For the big questions, the major theses, are sufficiently general and fundamental that they cannot be engaged directly. Indeed, it is difficult to see what engaging them directly might consist in. Rather, they must be explored carefully and gradually, through an examination of their presuppositions and their consequences. A philosophical encounter, like a military campaign, is fought on many fronts simultaneously; overall victory depends upon an extended series of tactical skirmishes and flanking maneuvers which inevitably and necessarily precede and lay the groundwork for any big push through the center. And not infrequently, when all these preparatory battles have been fought and won, the war is over. (Take another look at the quotation that forms the motto at the front of this book.)

Observation 2 accounts for the apparent *inconclusiveness* of philosophical disputes. Students of philosophy are frequently struck by the fact that philosophers seem to argue endlessly. Nothing new ever seems to happen; there appears to be no progress. Instead, the classical positions of major historical figures are continually being revived, refurbished, and refined.

But to the extent that this is true, it is not a shortcoming. Contemporary philosophers are not incapable of having new ideas. Rather, because the major stands on the large issues have generally already been mapped, the contemporary task often becomes one of attempting to work some of them into a coherent position. A contemporary contribution, then, often consists of the discovery of an unnoticed resourse of a traditional position or of a way to meet some objection long thought to be decisive against some classical philosophical strategy. A dispute between two philosophers will always, of course, be conducted against the background of some shared beliefs and presuppositions—and there is usually a third party waiting in the wings, prepared with arguments to challenge *them* . The hard fact of the matter is that systematic philosophical views have a staggering scope; one can hardly overestimate the magnitude of the task of tying together theses concerning knowledge, existence, truth, thought, language, action, and values into a coherent conceptual package. Quite often, as we will later have occasion to see, the trick is not to give answers, but to ask the right questions in the first place.

Observation 3 accounts for the apparent *pointlessness* of philosophical disputes. Philosophers seem stubbornly unwilling to settle down and talk about the issues, to recognize, admit, and make use of the facts. They just keep talking about one another's arguments. From outside the discipline, this looks like nothing so much as pointless domestic bickering. But you should now be in a position to appreciate that philosophical methodology demands this technique of confronting argument with argument precisely to *avoid* pointless bickering. Rule One, the requirement that criticism engage the argument, is exactly a response to the need for a method that is at least potentially *resolutive*, a method that can press beyond mere disagreement and apply the leverage of reasoning in a way which affords the possibility of rationally dislodging an entrenched philosophical thesis or view. The meeting of argument with argument is the essence of the matter. Unless criticism proceeded in this way, we would not yet have an activity of reason at all, but mere yea-saying and nay-saying—and that would be pointless bickering with a vengeance.

Rule One in Action: Refloating the Ship of Theseus

Recall, now, the state in which we left the dispute over Theseus's ship, the Spirit of Athens. We left ourselves with a pair of arguments. One philosopher, call him Xavier, is convinced that Theseus's ship is Ship X, the ship in dry-dock A at the end of the process. He offered us:

Argument X

1. The ship in Dock A at minute 0 is the Spirit of Athens.
2. Replacing one plank of a 1000-plank ship does not alter the identity of the ship.
3. The ship in Dock A at minute t differs from the ship in Dock A at minute 0 only in that one oak plank has been replaced by a teak plank.
4. So the ship in Dock A at minute t is the Spirit of Athens. [From 1, 2, 3]
5. The ship in Dock A at minute $2t$ differs from the ship in Dock A at minute t only in that one oak plank has been replaced by a teak plank.
6. So the ship in Dock A at minute $2t$ is the Spirit of Athens. [From 4, 2, 5]
7. But we can repeat this pattern of reasoning for minute $3t$, minute $4t$, minute $5t$, and so on, up to minute $1000t$, each repetition reaching the intermediate conclusion that the ship in Dock A at that time is the Spirit of Athens.
8. So the ship in Dock A at minute $1000t$ is the Spirit of Athens.
9. But Ship X is the ship in Dock A at minute $1000t$.
10. Hence, Ship X is Theseus's ship, the Spirit of Athens.

Another philosopher, in contrast—call her Yolanda—is convinced that it's Ship Y, the ship in dry-dock B at the end of the process, that's identical to the Spirit of Athens. She consequently offered us:

Argument Y:

1. A complex whole object (such as a ship) is nothing but the sum of its parts in a determinate arrangement.
2. The parts of Theseus's ship, the Spirit of Athens, are the 1000 sound and seaworthy oak planks of which it is composed at minute 0.
3. The parts of Ship Y are the 1000 sound and seaworthy oak planks of which *it* is composed at minute 1000t.
4. But every plank which is a part of Ship Y is (identical to) a plank which is a part of the Spirit of Athens.
5. Furthermore, the *arrangement* of the planks composing Ship Y is (plank-for-plank) identical to the arrangement of the planks composing the Spirit of Athens.
6. Hence, Ship Y *is* Theseus's ship, the Spirit of Athens. [From 1, 4, 5]

Criticism, Rule One tells us, must engage the arguments. Well, here are two arguments. How might their advocates proceed to criticize their opponents? What, in other words, could Yolanda say to Xavier *about his argument, Argument X?* And what, in contrast, might Xavier say to Yolanda *about her argument, Argument Y?*

At first blush, Argument X looks as though it will be pretty hard to fault. Apparently the only significant premise that the argument makes explicit is the one formulated in line 2—that replacing one plank of a 1000-plank ship does not alter the ship's identity—and, on the face of it, this is a claim that seems difficult to challenge. After all, if replacing one plank *did* alter the identity of the ship, then we'd never be able to *repair* such a ship by replacing a *damaged* plank with a sound new one. Instead of the ship we'd set out to repair, we'd wind up with a *different* ship—one for which, since it would no longer be identical to the ship we began with, we would presumably need new registry papers, licenses, and certificates of seaworthiness. If Yolanda rejects premise 2, in other words, she will evidently be abandoning the common-sense distinction between changing something *about* a ship (which continues to exist after the change) and creating a *new* ship (one which didn't exist until the change)—and this seems rather too drastic a price to pay.

But the *content* of Argument X is not the only thing about it that Yolanda might undertake to challenge. There is also its *form*. In particular, Argument X *reiterates* the application of the principle formulated in line 2—as line 7 makes clear, it is supposed to be applied repeatedly, plank after plank—and Yolanda might take issue with *this* procedure. That is, she might argue that although applying such a principle *once* is a valid argument form, applying it *repeatedly* is not. Doing *that*, she may claim, can lead from true premises to a false conclusion. One way to show this, as we know, is to construct a *model*, an argument having the same form, which *does* lead from true premises to a false conclusion.

With a little ingenuity, then, Yolanda might come up with something like this: Suppose that Homer is a bushy-headed man—he has, let's say, 10,000 hairs—and that we now begin once each minute to pluck exactly one hair from Homer's head. Yolanda then produces

Argument H:

1. At minute 0, Homer is bushy-headed and not bald.
2. Plucking one hair from the head of a bushy-headed man does not transform him from being bushy-headed to being bald.
3. But Homer at minute 1 differs from Homer at minute 0 only in that one hair has been plucked from his head.
4. So Homer at minute 1 is bushy-headed and not bald. [From 1, 2, 3]
5. But Homer at minute 2 differs from Homer at minute 1 only in that one more hair has been plucked from his head.
6. So Homer at minute 2 is bushy-headed and not bald. [From 4, 2, 5]
7. But we can repeat this pattern of reasoning for minute 3, minute 4, minute 5, and so on, up to minute 10,000, each repetition reaching the intermediate conclusion that Homer at that time is still bushy-headed and not bald.
8. So Homer at minute 10,000 is bushy-headed and not bald.

Given our initial assumption that Homer began with exactly 10,000 hairs on his head, however, the conclusion of *this* argument is patently false. This argument, in other words, proceeds from true premises to a false conclusion. Argument H is invalid. But, Yolanda continues, Argument X has the same form as Argument H. So Argument X is invalid. That's what's wrong with it. As this reasoning shows, there is something wrong with its *form*.

And what might Xavier have to say about Yolanda's original argument, Argument Y? Well, the significant new principle made explicit in that argument is surely the one formulated in line 1—that a complex whole is nothing but the sum of its parts in a determinate arrangement. Like the leading principle of Argument X, this premise, too, seems pretty commonsensical at first encounter. Nevertheless, Xavier could argue, it isn't quite right as it stands. He might remind us that some complex objects—automobiles, computers, and the like—have *replaceable* parts, and what that surely means is that the *object* persists through a *change* of some of its parts. This does not show that the complex thing is somehow mysteriously "more" than the sum of its parts in a determinate arrangement, but what it *does* show is that we need to *restrict* the application of that principle to specific *times*. Premise 1, he concludes, is imprecisely stated. It should read: "*At any given time*, a complex whole is nothing but the sum of its parts *at that time* in a determinate arrangement."

But once we have properly formulated its first premise, Xavier continues, we can see what is wrong with Yolanda's original argument, Argument Y: Another of its premises is not merely imprecisely formulated but simply false. The problem lies in line 4. It's just not true that every plank which is a part of Ship Y (at minute

1000t) is a plank which *is* a part of the Spirit of Athens. What's true is that every plank which is a part of Ship Y (at minute 1000t) is a plank which *was* a part of the Spirit of Athens *at minute 0*. In other words, being a part of Theseus's ship, the Spirit of Athens, is not an intrinsic property of a plank in the way its shape and size and weight are among its intrinsic properties, but simply an *episode* in the plank's career. A plank is a part of Theseus's ship only at certain *times*. Once it has been removed from the ship and replaced by another plank, however, it thereupon *ceases* to be a part of the Spirit of Athens. All that Yolanda is therefore entitled to say about the 1000 planks composing Ship Y at minute 1000t is that each is a *former* part of Theseus's ship, the Spirit of Athens; and we have *no* commonsensical principle that justifies a claim to the effect that a complex object at any given time is nothing but the sum of its *former* parts, however they might be arranged. Yolanda's argument (Argument Y), Xavier concludes, may indeed be valid, but the mere fact that it is *formally* in order does not commit us to accepting its conclusion. For there is still something wrong with it—and we can now say *what* is wrong with it. As this reasoning shows, there is something wrong with its *content*. It has a false premise.

Argument and counter-argument. Rule One in action. We began with two informal arguments about ships. We now have two new arguments—about arguments. The original question regarding the Spirit of Athens is not yet settled, but notice how the focus has shifted. To maintain his original stand, Xavier will now need to find an error in Yolanda's *new* reasoning—and this will require him, for instance, to search for *disanalogies* between the repeated application of a commonsensical principle regarding identity through change in his original Argument X, and Yolanda's repeated application of a commonsensical principle regarding bushy-headedness and baldness in her Argument H. Analogously, to maintain her original stand, Yolanda will need to search for challenges to the temporal restrictions which Xavier's new reasoning concludes must be imposed upon the part-whole relationship.

In this way, beginning from a small puzzle about ships, we can be led to rethink the vast topic of identity through change, and ultimately to systematize and make articulate our concepts of alteration and persistence, and of part and whole. This is Rule One in action. And if it does have its perils, it also has its joys—not the least of which is that it can, in principle, ultimately lead beyond mere disagreement.

The Joys and Perils of Dialectic

The points we've most recently been examining are sufficiently important to deserve a still more extensive discussion. We have seen that even in the most straightforward sort of case, where the acceptability of some claim is at issue, the methodology of philosophy already demands an elaborate sequential structure of competing arguments. A disagreement is transferred from conclusions to premises and from premises to presuppositions, ultimately pulling in whole complex families of beliefs and commitments. Much of what is initially disagreeable about the enterprise may become less so when seen in this light, that is, when the details of argument directed at seemingly inconsequential puzzles come to be appreciated as tactical moments in a larger philosophical development. Ultimately, any challenge is addressed not to this or that individual thesis but to the consistency and coherence of a whole family of beliefs in which the thesis is embedded.

What is genuinely at issue in a philosophical dispute, then, is not a particular statement or claim but rather a rich, more or less systematic *world view*. A philosophical encounter is like the collision of two icebergs. What lies beneath the surface is larger than, and gives shape and force to, what is visible above the waters. These philosophical world views have a special sort of comprehensiveness and elasticity. They shape our whole way of seeing the world. Opposition among them is *dialectical*.

Now the word 'dialectical' has had many uses in philosophy, from Plato to Marx. What I mean by it here is not unrelated to these historical roots. A pair of world views stand in what I call *dialectical opposition* just in case they are incompatible but nevertheless are both *tempting*, in that there's an initial pull toward each of them; both *pivotal*, in that they serve as centers for ordering and regrouping families of beliefs; and both *reformulatable*, in that they are expressible by a variety of different specific claims or theses.

Consider, for instance, what we might call the theistic and the nontheistic world views. Some people look at the world and see it as the perfect handiwork of a Divine creator, infused with a benevolent personal presence. Others greet this picture with incomprehension or hostility, seeing in the world only complex flows and interactions of mass and energy, the workings of blind and wholly impersonal forces. Perhaps most people have moments of both sorts from time to time, sometimes confronting the world with awe and reverence as a deep mystery, and sometimes confronting it as a mere object, imperfectly understood, to be sure, but in principle perfectly understandable and capable of someday being fully grasped and mastered.

Both pulls are undeniably there. Both pictures have an undeniable attraction for us. But it is clear that, even with the most prodigious efforts at self-deception, one cannot retain both pictures indefinitely at the same time. They are ultimately incompatible with one another.

How is this incompatibility to be expressed? One traditional way, of course, is as a disagreement over the *statement* "God exists." One philosopher offers an argument for or against the statement; another replies with criticisms of that argument; the first responds to the criticism of the second with a critique of his own; still other voices enter the chorus; and so it goes. But to see this ongoing dialogue as a dispute concerned only with the truth or falsehood of a single statement is to overlook the greater hidden mass of the icebergs.

For, in an important sense, everything is touched by the issue. One of these disputants, for example, lives in a universe permeated with meaning. This universe, and we within it, have a purpose, exist for a reason. For the other disputant, in contrast, if there are to be meanings and purposes at all they must be *human* meanings and purposes, for we are here not by design but as the result of the random coming together of appropriate raw materials and the systematic evolutionary working out of this original fortuitous chance concurrence.

Again, one philosopher sees people as "a little lower than the angels"—as creatures who are imbued with souls and with a Divine spark of life, who are granted the freedom to choose between good and evil in accordance with or in opposition to

God's will. For the other, however, we are perhaps only "a little higher than the apes"—sophisticated deterministic organic data-processors which create whatever values there are in the process of our mutual interactions and our continuing adaptation to a universe of value-free, uncaring stuff. For one, death is a transition to a higher life; for the other, it is only the ultimate, irreversible malfunction.

Any of these differences, and many others, can emerge as a focal point from which the dialectical process of meeting argument with argument then develops. People have souls—or they do not. There is life after death—or there is not. We have free will—or we are determined. There are ultimate values—or all values are conventional. Sensory perception is our only knowledge-yielding faculty—or mystical experience gives us access to a higher reality. Whatever the specific *thesis*, the ultimate aim of the enterprise remains the same: to assemble from pieces rooted in the preferred picture a consistent, coherent, articulate, and systematic whole that can stand the test of critical challenge, to build a synthesis that hangs together under analysis.

From time to time, the center shifts. A thesis is reformulated. To the beginner this looks like yet another step in an endless and inconclusive process of regeneration of arguments. But, oddly enough, it is progress. With each such reformulation, more of what is at issue comes to light, more of the iceberg emerges from the water. Often the trick is to ask the right questions. Each shift of the center gives us more good questions to ask.

Even when the center remains fixed, from time to time the focus shifts. Argument turns to details and minutiae. Pointless hairsplitting, thinks the beginner. But this too is progress. For a complex and systematic philosophical world view does not simply fall to pieces. It has too much resilience for that. If inconsistency and incoherence are to be found at all, they will reveal themselves precisely in these fine points, in the inability of the whole to accommodate a telling criticism of some minute part.

That is how philosophical progress is made. And that is why it is so difficult to recognize. The dialectical process of philosophy proceeds by meeting argument with argument. Each criticism is a probe directed at a world view from within, a challenge to its *internal* coherence and consistency, framed by one who stands himself outside it. And each response embodies the mutual adjustment of manifold beliefs, presuppositions, commitments, and convictions, an attempt to fine-tune the larger conceptual substructure which supports the visible thesis.

By now you may be despairing of ever entering into the practice of philosophy in a significant way. How can one so much as *begin* a process of argumentation which draws in these ways upon such complicated systematic philosophical world views? Well, it's time for a bit of good news. You yourself already have at least the beginnings of such a complicated systematic philosophical world view. It's what you sometimes think of as "common sense."

Now a word of caution is immediately in order. Common sense of course includes a good bit of common nonsense as well, and one person's common sense is sometimes another's insanity. Nevertheless, there remains considerable shared territory under the banner of common sense, and this in particular is what I have in mind. Within this shared territory fall such beliefs as these: that the world contains a variety of things—objects, plants, animals, and people; that the things in the world have various properties—shapes, sizes, and colors, for example—and exhibit various behaviors—some grow and some move, for instance; that these things act on and interact with one another; that we know about many of these things and about their interactions—we have encountered some of them, seen or heard or tasted them, and figured out that there must be others we haven't met; and that we ourselves think and speak and act in this world, and that our words and actions often have consequences, some of which are desirable and some undesirable.

All these beliefs, and many others, are what I think of as "common sense." Common sense of this kind is everybody's starting place, and so it will be yours. But the fundamental rules of the philosophical enterprise still apply. The fact that some philosophical thesis runs counter to such common sense is just one of those disagreements that serves as a beginning from which the dialectical process of meeting argument with argument must then proceed. Common sense is not inviolate. It is not a final court of appeals. Even at its best, it is only one philosophical standpoint among the many that are possible. Indeed, *every one* of the "common-sense" beliefs that I listed above has, in fact, been challenged—and for compelling reasons—by some philosopher of the past.

And common sense has its liabilities. One typically does not have the experience of putting its contents to the test of critical scrutiny. Since the loose but interconnected set of concepts, beliefs, theories, and principles that constitute such common sense are shared operative presuppositions of our everyday life, they are not often challenged in the ordinary course of that everyday life. Indeed, part of what students often find so infuriating about philosophical inquiry is just the philosopher's refusal to defer to and be content with common sense. It, too, must be put to the test of argument. And again, precisely because it is *not* commonly put to that test, one typically does not know how to fully articulate, much less systematically organize, its complex implicit structure of presuppositions and conceptual connections. Nor is one entirely sure of how much confidence to place in its ultimate internal coherence.

But as a starting place, such common sense has its assets, too. For one thing, you're at home in it. You can usually recognize common sense when you hear it. For another, it has something very important going for it—it works. The conceptual scheme of common sense is generally a useful, practical framework within which to conduct our everyday lives and carry out our activities, and this surely creates at least the presumption that there is *something* right about it.

That common sense can and does function in this way as a more or less systematic and understandable stock of beliefs, theories, and principles that can be drawn upon in critical or constructive argumentation captures what truth there is to the view that "everyone has a philosophy." But it does not follow from this that everyone is a philosopher. The decisive step toward that goal is made when one stops taking common sense for granted and begins to put it to the test. Recall Aristotle: "Philosophy begins in wonder." The great philosophers of the past represent, among their other virtues, some of the most forceful, dramatic, and articulate challenges to our common-sense world view. And that is another reason why we still study their arguments today and are likely to do so for all of our tomorrows.

First Intermission

It's time to pause and take a deep breath.

What I've been doing in the preceding chapters is sketching out one conception of the philosophical enterprise—its goals, its methods, and the manner in which it progresses. The picture I've been drawing is of philosophy as a "second-order" discipline, aimed not at enriching our knowledge of the world in which we find ourselves but at the critical examination of our reasoned engagement with that world; philosophy as the rational survey of our rational practices in the natural and behavioral sciences, the arts and humanities, and indeed in everyday life as well. In this picture, the goal of philosophy is essentially to achieve a synthetic and synoptic *overview* of our place in the world, a coherent and comprehensive understanding of our abilities and limitations as rational knowers of that world and rational agents within it.

As we have seen, however, philosophical inquiry viewed *close up* frequently fails to reveal such systematic and global aims. On the contrary, philosophical inquiry in detail often appears trivial, inconclusive, and pointless—a series of sterile and irrelevant logical quibbles. I have also argued, however, that these appearances are in reality *consequences* of the "second-order" character of philosophical inquiry, and, in particular, of the *method* which philosophy's unique nature as a discipline inevitably demands.

That method is what I have described as "dialectic." Its tools are *arguments*, and its essential procedure is the critical engagement *of* arguments *with* arguments. We have, indeed, spent a good bit of time examining these rational tools and their application. We have seen that a critical challenge can be addressed either to the form of a piece of reasoning or to its content, either to the question of validity or to the truth of the premises. We have met a variety of common argument forms, both valid princes and invalid frogs, and explored the technique of *modeling* by means of which validity can be called into question. And we have described the process of *internal* criticism demanded by the dialectical and systematic character of philosophical views, theses, or positions—a process that ultimately challenges the *coherence* of some whole complex interrelated *system* of beliefs within which any specific philosophical claim is necessarily and inevitably embedded.

Throughout this discussion, I have continually emphasized what I call Rule One, the requirement that philosophical criticism engage the arguments—that is, that it address not just the problematic *conclusions* at which some philosopher arrives but rather the *inner workings* of the pieces of reasoning by means of which he or she arrives at those conclusions. Only such a method, I have argued, holds out even the hope of *resolving* a philosophical disagreement. Whether one's critical strategy be the internal criticism of premises or the technique of modeling, then, what is crucial is that a philosophical challenger is invariably called upon to *produce* an argument of his or her own—a process that we have, in fact, seen in action in our short study of the "Ship of Theseus" puzzle. One philosophical view, then, is inevitably challenged from the standpoint of *another;* and I have suggested, finally, that the loose confederation of concepts, beliefs, theories, and principles that I called "common sense" itself implicitly constitutes such a systematic philosophical stance from which a student can begin—although, as with any such stance, "common sense" too is open to exploration, articulation, and critical philosophical challenge.

These, then, are the aims, the methods, and some of the complexities of the practice of philosophy. Philosophy, it turns out, is not a mere random clash of personal opinions but a coherent *discipline* with its own unique intellectual goals, conceptual tools, and rational strategies. With a preliminary understanding of those goals, tools, and strategies now in hand, we can proceed to consider those larger structures within which those goals are sought, those tools put to use, and those strategies pursued—that is, to consider philosophical inquiry in the forms in which you will encounter it and in which you yourself will be asked to attempt it. We can now turn, in other words, to the topic which in many ways is the centerpiece and motivating idea of this book, the *philosophical essay.*

CHAPTER SIX

Philosophical Essays: Critical Examination of a View

The primary medium for working through a philosophical dialectic is the philosophical essay. This is a distinctive form which ranges from brief discussion notes in professional journals to works of book length. As a student of philosophy, you will (or should) be called upon to try your hand at writing philosophical essays. In any case, you will surely be reading some, and so a thorough discussion of the form is appropriate here.

A philosophical essay is neither a research paper, a scholarly collection and arrangement of diverse sources (although the standards and forms of scholarly documentation should, of course, be observed whenever relevant and necessary), nor is it a literary exercise in self-expression. It does not deal with feelings or impressions. It is not a report or a summary. Fundamentally, it is the *reasoned defense of a thesis*. That is, there must be some point or points to be *established* in the essay, and considerations must be offered in *support* of them in such a way that the considerations can be seen *to* support them.

Clarity of exposition, precision of statement, organization of ideas, and logical rigor and consistency in the treatment of those ideas are thus among the primary demands of philosophical writing. It follows that literacy and sound literary style are essential preconditions of a successful philosophical essay (indeed, I would add, of *any* writing). At a minimum, a philosophical essay should be written in coherent and articulate prose which adheres to the accepted rules and conventions of English grammar and composition. Enthusiasm cannot compensate for unintelligibility, nor can a superficial facility with technical terms effectively substitute for a sound understanding of the ideas and principles that such terminology has evolved to express. You should particularly avoid ponderous "academic" forms. Philosophy has had a bad press in this regard. It is notorious for being a "deep" subject, and those who write about it all too often aspire to a corresponding impenetrability. Well, deep philosophy may be—but the deep lucidity of a glacier-fed mountain lake, not the deep murkiness of a mist-laden swamp, should be your model and inspiration.

Philosophical essays come in a variety of *species*, each of which has its own characteristic structure. Perhaps the most basic of these, mastery of which serves as a point of entry to all the others, is the critical examination of a view.

The critical examination of a view, of course, presupposes a view to be critically examined. That is, you are confronted at the beginning with something that *itself* has fundamentally the form of a philosophical essay—a piece of writing within which some claim or thesis is advanced and considerations are offered in favor of accepting or adopting that claim. Correspondingly, a critical examination of a view may be broadly divided into two parts: the exposition and the critique. Exposition consists in setting out for study and discussion the view, position, claim, or thesis at issue together with the structure of argumentation offered in support of it. Critique is the assessment or evaluation of that view through an examination of the structure and content of the supporting reasoning. One useful way to approach the writing of such a philosophical essay, then, is with something like the following checklist of questions in mind:[1]

Introduction:

Does my essay have an introductory paragraph?
In my introductory paragraph, do I

__ give a brief description of what the essay is about?

__ state what I plan to accomplish in the essay?

__ summarize how I plan to go about accomplishing it?

The Exposition:

When reconstructing an argument, have I clearly explained

__ what conclusion the philosopher is working toward?

__ what reasons, both implicit and explicit, the philosopher offers to support that conclusion?

__ why and how the philosopher thinks those reasons support the conclusion?

The Critique:

When raising an objection, have I

__ made it clear what aspect of the argument I object to?

__ explained the reasons why I object to that aspect of the argument?

---

[1] Adapted from a helpful set of notes about writing philosophy papers produced for the Writing Center at the University of North Carolina, Chapel Hill, by Jane Reid, one of my exceptionally talented teaching assistants.

___ assessed the severity of my objection?

___ thought about and discussed how the philosopher might respond to my objection?

___ discussed one objection thoroughly rather than many objections superficially?

General Concerns:

Throughout my paper, do I periodically tell the reader

___ what I've just done?

___ what remains to be done?

___ what the reader should expect to happen next?

___ whether what I am saying is an interpretation or a criticism?

Does my essay have a clear and articulate structure?

___ Does each paragraph work to support my thesis?

___ Do I have transitions between paragraphs that make it clear why one paragraph follows the one which precedes it?

___ Does each sentence within a paragraph work to support or explain the topic of that paragraph?

Have I satisfactorily explained

___ any important special terminology that the author employs?

___ the interpretation of any passages that I quote?

___ the nature and point of any examples that I offer?

As helpful as such a brief checklist can often be, however, both the idea of a philosophical exposition and, especially, the topic of a philosophical critique deserve a more extensive discussion.

Views are usually somebody's views. The expository task is thus primarily exegetical. The business of setting out a position together with its supporting argumentation will usually be a matter of reading, understanding, reconstructing, and lucidly reporting the content of some philosophical work. This undertaking has its own strategies and hazards, some of which I will have occasion to discuss later.

As I have repeatedly stressed, the most important fact about a philosophical critique is that it does not end with disagreement. That is where it begins. Philosophical criticism is *reasoned* disagreement. Since the view up for assessment will be supported by its own structure of reasoned considerations, a negative philosophical evaluation of a thesis requires that the arguments supporting the position, and not merely the position itself, be critically engaged. That's Rule One. It is, you will recall, thus never sufficient simply to point out that a philosophical conclusion looks, or even is, false or paradoxical. If you wish effectively to call the conclusion into question, what you need to discover and demonstrate are the inadequacies of the reasoning offered in support of it.

As we have seen, there are two directions which a critical thrust can take. You may address the form of the argument—its validity or invalidity—or you may address its content. I have already said most of what can usefully be said about the first type of criticism outside the confines of a course in formal logic. The exposition of the argument to be evaluated is clearly crucial to this mode of criticism. The argument must be set out with sufficient clarity and precision and in sufficient orderly detail to allow for the extraction of a "logical skeleton" that in fact fairly and accurately represents the pattern of reasoning actually being employed. Unfortunately, nothing short of the kind of familiarity and practice that only repeated experience brings suffices to indicate what the argument is likely to be and how much detail is needed to uncover its operative logical structure. Even if you've successfully accomplished this rather tough job, however, your ability to demonstrate the argument's invalidity (if it *is* invalid) is still limited by your insight in recognizing it for what it is, and by your creativity in coming up with an appropriate model to *demonstrate* invalidity by exhibiting a further instance of that pattern of reasoning with indisputably true premises and an indisputably false conclusion. Alas, as I remarked earlier, both insight and creativity sadly fall outside the limits of what is teachable.

Usually, however, you will be dealing with patterns of reasoning that are formally correct. In that case, your critique will need to address the specific content of the argument. The way you do this, you surely remember, is to construct an *internal* criticism. That is, you attempt to establish that the various premises and presuppositions used in the argument cannot all consistently be held together. You try to show that anyone who accepts all of those premises and presuppositions at the same time—and in particular, then, the philosopher who offered the argument in the first place—lands in trouble.

What kind of trouble? I have repeatedly spoken of uncovering an inconsistency or an incoherence in some philosopher's views. It is now time to talk about this matter in more detail. What kinds of incoherence or inconsistency are there? And what do they look like when you uncover them?

In a sense, there is only one *basic* form of inconsistency or incoherence—a self-contradiction. In the most straightforward case, a person contradicts himself by saying two things which cannot both be true at the same time. At one point in the dialectic he says X; at another, he says *not-X*. In a somewhat less straightforward case, however, he may, so to speak, say both X and *not-X* at the same time. This sounds a bit mysterious, but in fact you've already seen at least one example of it. A person who claimed that all paintings were forgeries would be contradicting himself in this way, for he would in effect be saying both that some paintings are originals (for the forgeries to be copies of) and that no paintings are originals, both X and *not-X*.

Roughly, a claim is self-contradictory if it is false and its falsehood can be determined using *only* facts about the meanings of the words used to express the claim.[2] "Some parents have no children," "Tom is taller than Sam, who is taller than Tom," "Mary can draw a four-sided triangle," "John is his own father's uncle," and "Yesterday I met a married bachelor" are examples of claims which it is plausible to regard as in this sense self-contradictory.

Of course, philosophers are rarely polite enough to supply you with even this straightforward a self-contradiction. More often the inconsistency, if there is one, will be merely *implicit*. The philosopher won't *say* both *X* and *not-X*. Instead, he'll say *X*, and also say a lot of other things—*U, V, W, Y, Z*—which, taken together, *imply not-X*. This is, in fact, the typical case, and so it's the one that I outlined earlier when I first introduced the notion of internal criticism.

Your job as a critic, correspondingly, is to make such an implicit contradiction *explicit*. As we have seen, you do this by constructing an argument of your own, one whose premises are claims that the philosopher under examination accepts—*U, V, W, Y, Z*—and whose conclusion is something that he's on record as being committed to reject—*not-X*. A main part of your critical task, then, is to draw out and exhibit the implications of what is explicitly said in the work you are criticizing. And that is another reason why fair and accurate exposition necessarily precedes an effective critique. You can't determine what a person's explicit views *imply* until you've first gotten properly clear about what those views in fact *are*.

But we're still not finished exploring the variety of subtle ways that a stretch of philosophical argumentation can embody a conceptual incoherence. So far, I have been talking only about contradictions between what is said and what is said or implied. In a sophisticated piece of philosophical reasoning, however, the inconsistency, if there is one, may well lie not even that close to the surface. What a philosopher explicitly says, that is, will very often contradict neither anything else that he explicitly says nor even anything *implied by* the other things he explicitly says. Nevertheless, what he says may still contradict something else to which he is *committed*, not by saying it or implying it but, for instance, by simply taking it for granted or *presupposing* it.

Everyone, of course, takes many things for granted all the time, and practicing philosophers are no exception. Some of the things taken for granted are what we might call *implicit premises*, claims that are regarded as being so obviously true that they are just never mentioned. They "go without saying." Uncovering such implicit premises is often a tricky job, rather like diagnosing the motive behind some act, but once they've been brought out into the open they behave just like explicit premises.

---

[2] My occasional cautionary phrases, such as 'in effect' and 'roughly', mark the locus of a philosophical problem that has, in fact, grown into a full-fledged philosophical dialectic, ultimately encompassing views concerning meaning, truth, reference, knowledge, necessity, linguistics, and even natural science. The issue is a complicated one, but the gist of it is that some philosophers have argued that the sort of notion of self-contradiction that I have sketched is ill-defined and, in particular, that it draws upon a picture of *meaning* which is itself incoherent and unacceptable. As befits an introductory text, I shall, apart from this note, continue to be casual and intuitive about the matter. If you are interested in pursuing the problem, however, one place to begin is with the section called "Analyticity" in Jay F. Rosenberg and Charles Travis, eds., *Readings in the Philosophy of Language* (Englewood Cliffs, NJ: Prentice-Hall, Inc., 1971).

You work out their implications in conjunction with those of other things the philosopher says, and you attempt to exhibit the incoherence, if there is one, in the form of an explicit self-contradiction.

But even beyond implicit premises that may or may not be lurking behind a particular argument, there are some other things that are necessarily presupposed or taken for granted in the course of *any* argument. These are what you might think of as the most general ground rules for all constructive reasoning. I shall call them "canons of rational practice." Canons of rational practice incorporate the fundamental constraints that must be adhered to in order to have any coherent argument at all—good or bad, valid or invalid. A specifically *philosophical* sort of criticism— and one which often proves especially puzzling to the beginner—is to attempt to convict the person who has ostensibly offered an argument of violating one of *these*. And someone who *has* violated one of the canons of rational practice has produced something incoherent, all right, but in a special way. He hasn't exactly contradicted *himself*. Instead, he has contradicted the presumption that what he's offering is an argument suitable for establishing its conclusion—or any conclusion at all. He has, so to speak, subtly opted out of the reasoning game. But all this is still awfully general and vague. Examples of such canons of rational practice and their violation, spelled out in some detail, are clearly what we need. That, consequently, is my next project. I shall, in fact, supply five.

Five Ways to Criticize a Philosopher

1. Equivocation

William James reported returning from a walk to find a group of friends debating about a squirrel clinging to the trunk of a tree. As someone walked around the tree, it seemed, the canny squirrel edged sideways around the trunk, always keeping it between himself and the moving person. James's friends were quite sure that the person went around the tree. What they couldn't seem to agree about was whether the person went around the squirrel. Here's how James dealt with the question:

> "Which party is right," I said, "depends on what you *practically mean* by 'going around' the squirrel. If you mean passing from the north of him to the east, then to the south, then to the west, and then to the north of him again, obviously the man does go around him, for he occupies these successive positions. But if on the contrary you mean being first in front of him, then on the right of him, then behind him, then on his left, and finally in front again, it is quite as obvious that the man fails to go round him, for by the compensating movements the squirrel makes, he keeps his belly turned towards the man all the time, and his back turned away. Make the distinction, and there is no occasion for any further dispute."[1]

The moral of this story is that whether a particular claim is true or false always depends, among other things, on how the words used to formulate it are to be interpreted. Often, as in this instance, some key word or phrase will be *ambiguous*, admitting of a variety of *readings*, and the same sentence can be used to say something true when read in one way and something false when read in another.

Now it frequently happens that such a word or phrase crops up several times in the course of an argument. It may occur in several premises, and perhaps also in the conclusion. Whether the argument is a good one will, of course, then depend, among other things, on how you interpret that word or phrase. If you read it one way, the

---

[1] William James, *Essays in Pragmatism* (New York, N.Y.: Hafner, 1948), p. 141.

premises may come out true; if you read it another way, they may come out false. The philosopher offering the argument, it is reasonable to suppose, wants all the premises to come out true. Sometimes, however, the only way to accomplish this is to read the key word or phrase one way in one premise and a *different* way in another premise. To do this is to violate one of what I'm calling the canons of rational practice. It is to *equivocate*. A word must mean the same thing every time it occurs in a single argument. That's the canon at issue. To violate it is, in effect, to change the subject in mid-argument.

Here's a transparent, simple-minded (and sexist) example of equivocation in action:
At first blush, the argument appears to be formally impeccable. Since its conclusion

(1)	Only men can speak rationally.
(2)	No woman is a man.
(3)	So, no woman can speak rationally.

is plainly false, however, there must be a problem with its content. One of its premises must be false. But which one? That depends upon how you read them!

The key term is obviously 'men'. Premise (1), we might argue, is true: Dogs, apes, goldfish, flatworms, carrots, and the like cannot speak at all, and although parrots, for instance, do speak, they do not speak rationally but only echo a limited number of phrases that they've been taught. So only men can speak rationally. Arguing in this way, we contrast "men" with members of other *species*. We're reading 'men', in other words, as equivalent to 'human beings'—but on this reading, of course, premise (2) is false. Women are certainly human beings. Alternatively, if we make premise (2) true by reading 'men' as equivalent to 'males', premise (1) becomes false. Crucially, there is no *single* reading for 'men' according to which premises (1) and (2) *both* come out true at the same time. And that is equivocation.

What we have in equivocation is, in fact, an interplay between form and content. The validity of the argument is *itself* incompatible with the simultaneous truth of both its premises. So we can, in a sense, choose what has gone wrong. Suppose we want to regard the argument as formally valid. We can do that. We need only view it as having the following skeleton:
Putting the same letter A in both (1*) and (2*) signals that whatever word or phrase

(1*)	Only A's are B.
(2*)	No C is an A.
(3*)	So, no C is a B.

replaces it is to be read in the same way on each of its occurrences. But if we do that in our original argument, as we've just seen, one of the premises will be false.

Conversely we can, if we wish, treat the argument as having a flawless *content* by choosing readings which make both premises come out true. That is, we can treat the argument as if what it said was:

(1')	Only human beings can speak rationally.
(2')	No woman is a male.
(3')	So, no woman can speak rationally.

In this case, however, the relevant logical skeleton of the argument would become:

(1†)	Only *A*'s are *B*.
(2†)	No *C* is a *D*.
(3†)	So, no *C* is a *B*.

and this is a patently invalid form. (Indeed, the argument from the true premises (1´) and (2´) to the false conclusion (3´) is just the model we need in order to exhibit its invalidity, isn't it?)

So what's wrong with the original argument? Is it invalid? Well, it is *if* we read both premises as true. Is there a false premise, then? Well, there is *if* we regard the argument as having a valid form. What's wrong with the argument is that its validity is itself incompatible with the simultaneous truth of its premises—and that violates a canon of rational practice. What's wrong with the argument is that it *equivocates* on

(a)	A necessary truth is true.
(b)	Whatever is true is possibly true.
(c)	Whatever is possibly true could be false.
(d)	So, a necessary truth could be false.

the key term 'men'. And now it's time for a full-fledged philosophical example:[2]
But, of course, a necessary truth cannot possibly be false. Something seems to have gone wrong. But what?

Let's think about it. Formally, the argument *seems* to be in good shape. It looks valid. (To be sure, this is no guarantee that it *is* valid.) Perhaps one of its premises is false. How about (a)? It looks okay. If some claim is *necessarily* true, then it's surely true. What about (b)? Again, there doesn't seem to be any obvious problem. If a claim actually *is* true, then it certainly *could be* true. It would be self-contradictory to say that the same claim both is true and couldn't possibly be true. If it weren't even *possibly* true, then it would *have* to be false. But no claim can be both true and false. So if some claim is actually true, it must be possibly true as well. That leaves (c) — but, alas, it also appears to be in pretty good shape. To say that a claim is possibly true is to say, not that it *is* true, but only that it *could be*. It could be true—but it could also be false. (It couldn't, of course, be both.) Consider, for example, the claim: The snow was heavy on Mount Kilamanjaro this year. That, we might say, is possibly true. It

---

2 Taken from Paul Weiss, "The Paradox of Necessary Truth," *Philosophical Studies* 6, 1955, pp. 31–2. You may be wondering, by the way, why any philosopher would *offer* such an argument as this. Well, one motive might be to show that there's something wrong with the notions of necessity and possibility, that the notions *themselves* incorporate some conceptual incoherence. Weiss's own motives, which have something to do with "illegitimate abstraction", are fairly obscure.

could be true—but it could also be false. Even if it *is* true, it still *could have been* false (if, for instance, the winds had shifted in certain ways). If we say that it *couldn't* be false that the snow was heavy on Mount Kilamanjaro this year, then we'd surely have to conclude that it *has to be* true, that it's a *necessary* truth. But surely whether or not it snowed heavily on Mount Kilamanjaro in a given year is not a matter of necessity but always just a matter of fact. So it looks as if (c) is also in order. A claim that's possibly true could be false. What, then, is wrong with the argument?

The best thing to do at this point is to abandon the argument for a moment and think about what we already know about necessity and truth. Before we began puzzling over the premises of this argument, we were inclined to sort claims into four groups. First, of course, we could divide them into the true ones and the false ones. But each of these groups, in turn, can be subdivided. Among the true claims, we were prepared to distinguish those which were necessarily true (couldn't be false) from those which were *contingently* true, true as a matter of fact (but which might have been false). Similarly, among the false claims, we distinguished those which were necessarily false (self-contradictory) from those which were *contingently* false, false as a matter of fact (but which might have been true). These classifications give us the following scheme:

	NECESSARY	**CONTINGENT**
TRUE	**NT:** Necessarily True (e.g., "A square has four sides.")	**CT:** Contingently True (e.g., "Some tables are made of metal.")
FALSE	**NF:** Necessarily False (e.g., "George's grandfather had no children.")	**CF:** Contingently False (e.g., "No-one has ever been killed by an atomic explosion.")

Now we can can return to the argument. The question we need to ask is this: Which of these four groups contain claims that are *possibly true?* Once we've carefully sorted things out this way, however, it becomes clear that there are a couple of different answers. It depends, one might say, on what we *mean* by 'possibly true'. If all we mean is *not necessarily false*, then all of the groups NT, CT, and CF will contain claims that are "possibly true." On this interpretation, only NF is excluded. But if, instead, we mean *contingently true,* then only the group CT will contain claims that are "possibly true." Interpreting 'possibly true' in this way excludes not just NF, but NT and CF as well. There are, in other words, two readings of the key phrase 'possibly true'. But which one does the author of the argument have in mind?

The answer, of course, is both. He *equivocates* between them. Premise (b) comes out true only if we read 'possibly true' in the first way, as equivalent to 'not necessarily false'—but on that reading, premise (c) will be false. On the other hand, we can regard premise (c) as true by reading 'possibly true' in the second way, as equivalent to 'contingently true'—but on that reading, premise (b) will be false. There is, in short, no *single* reading of 'possibly true' for which *both* premise (b) *and* premise (c) come out true at the same time. And so the argument sins against the canons of rational practice. Its validity is incompatible with the simultaneous truth of its premises. Its author is guilty of equivocation. And that is one way to criticize a philosopher.

2.   *Question Begging*

"But you can't just *assume* that! That's what you're trying to *prove*!" is a lament that one sometimes encounters in the casual coffee-shop disputations of daily life. At stake is another canon of rational practice: An argument must not beg the question. The root notion is easy enough to set out in a rough and ready way, but more difficult to make precise. Briefly and crudely put, an argument begs the question if it uses its conclusion as a premise.

What's wrong with such an argument? Well, according to the diagnostic scheme that we've developed so far, if there is a fault, it ought to lie either in the form or in the content. Now it's obvious that no question-begging argument is going to be formally invalid. Since any statement follows from itself, an argument that uses some statement as a premise (with or without purporting to use other premises) and then derives that very statement as its conclusion must be valid. It's impossible for all the premises to be true and the conclusion false for the simple reason that one of the premises *is* the conclusion, and no statement can be both true and false.

The problem with a question-begging argument, then, must lie with the content. However, the problem in this case is not our *ordinary* problem of content. Normally we criticize the content of an argument on the grounds that one of its premises is false. But can we do that here? The key premise is plainly the one which is also the conclusion. The only way to challenge the argument is to challenge *it*. (Since any statement already follows from itself, any other premises are simply superfluous. They do no logical work.) Well, then, is the key premise false? Essentially the answer is: We don't know. More precisely, since the key premise is identical to the conclusion, the question "Is the key premise false?" is the *same question* as "Is the conclusion false?"

At this point, it's especially important to remember that every philosophical argument occurs in a dialectical context. There are two parties to the dispute. One is the critic, who disputes the conclusion at issue. He believes that it is false. The other is the arguer. She accepts the conclusion at issue, presumably believing it to be true. So far, however, we have only a difference of opinion. The methodology of philosophy, and, in particular, Rule One, exists precisely to provide the possibility of *resolving* such a disagreement. It requires that the proponent of a thesis provide an argument for her view, that she produce considerations in support of it; and it requires that a critic who wishes to challenge that thesis address his challenge not to the view alone but directly to the argument, to the structure of reasoning that supposedly supports the view. Clearly, then, it is a presupposition of this *method* that a challenge to the argument supporting a conclusion must be *different* from a challenge to its conclusion; a criticism of the argument supporting a conclusion must differ from a mere disagreement with the conclusion. What we need to do is turn this observation on its head: It is a presupposition of the methodology of philosophy that something *qualifies as an argument in support of a conclusion* only if a challenge to what's supposed to do the supporting is different from a challenge to what's supposed to be supported.

Now we can say what's wrong with a question-begging argument: A philosopher who offers such an argument contradicts a presupposition of the very method which he or she professes to employ. What is offered as an argument in support of a conclusion does not qualify as such an argument according to the methodological requirements of the philosophical discipline he or she is supposed to be practicing. It does not qualify as such an argument because, as we have seen, the only way to challenge the supposed reasoning is to question its key premise, and doing that cannot be distinguished from merely challenging the ostensible argument's conclusion. The philosopher who advances such an argument, then, *cannot* be respecting Rule One; he or she has, so to speak, opted out of the dialectical game.

Of course, a philosopher is rarely unsophisticated enough to take the intended conclusion of some line of reasoning as an *explicit* premise—and that makes criticizing an argument as being question-begging a difficult and subtle business. If the conclusion is used as a premise at all, it is much more likely to be merely *implicit* in the argument. And as I have already noted, unearthing implicit premises is a sensitive matter of conceptual archaeology, requiring the sort of insightful understanding of forms of argument that comes only through extended practice and familiarity.

The issue of question begging is further complicated by the fact that there is *a* sense in which the conclusion of any good argument is "contained in" its premises. It is "contained in" them precisely in the sense that it is *implied by* them. If the premises are true, the conclusion must also be true. Thus, for valid arguments, *settling* the question of the truth of the premises always counts as *settling* the question of the truth of the conclusion. One must take special care not to confuse this coinciding of *answers* with the identity of *questions* that constitutes the fallacy of begging the question.

Indeed, it is even sometimes dialectically appropriate to take as a premise some claim which is *logically equivalent* to the intended conclusion. Two statements are logically equivalent just in case they imply one another. For example, the two statements

Every four-legged animal has fur.
No animal with four legs fails to have fur.

are logically equivalent, and so are these two:

If we invite Jon, we've got to invite Susan too.
We can't invite Jon unless we also invite Susan.

If either member of one of these pairs is true, it follows that the other member of the pair is true as well. In this sense, they "say the same thing."

It will be dialectically appropriate to take one of a pair of logically equivalent statements as a premise and the other as a conclusion just in case the point of the argument is to *demonstrate* the supposed logical equivalence itself. Such an argument frequently occurs within the critical movement of the dialectic. A critic attempts to establish that some philosopher has indeed contradicted himself by trying to show that something the philosopher has *accepted* is in fact equivalent to something he's *rejected.* The critic thus takes one of the claims at issue as a premise and attempts to exhibit a series of valid moves which transform it into the other claim. She intends the premise and conclusion of her argument to "say the same thing" because her proposed *dialectical* conclusion is that they *do* "say the same thing." Her derivation of the logically equivalent conclusion, then, is not the *end* of her critical reasoning, but actually only a stop along the way toward establishing her overall critical claim—that the premise and conclusion of her first-level argument *are* logically equivalent. This second-level claim about the logical equivalence of two statements, the critic's *dialectical* conclusion, then, is what in turn the original philosopher must challenge. And a challenge to this conclusion is *not* a challenge to the leading premise of the critic's first-level argument—indeed, the first philosopher has already accepted *that* premise in his *original* argument—but rather a challenge to the argument's form, to the validity of the moves that are supposed to establish the claimed logical equivalence. Despite appearances, then, the critic's argument in such a case is not question begging after all. (And appearances can be very deceptive here. Most philosophers aren't as explicit—or as clear—as they ought to be about what they're up to dialectically.)

This observation highlights, perhaps as well as anything can, the crucial importance of the *dialectical setting* of a philosophical argument. That is yet another reason why the history of philosophy is methodologically central to its practice. It exhibits philosophical theses in a variety of diverse dialectical environments. And as we have just seen, the same thesis—indeed, even the same argument—can be subject to quite different interpretations and assessments in different dialectical settings. (We'll encounter some additional examples of this phenomenon shortly.)

For the reasons I've just been discussing, genuine examples of question-begging philosophical arguments are not very easy to come by. Perhaps we can find one such example, however, in some argumentation surrounding the classical problem of *induction.*

In one of its guises, the problem of induction concerns our grounds for forming reasonable expectations about the future. All of us in fact have such expectations, and it seems that we characteristically form them by generalizing from our past experiences. The sun has risen regularly each day, the traditional example goes, and so, unless we have some quite special reason to think otherwise, it is reasonable to expect it to go on doing so. We expect water to stay liquid at temperatures above zero degrees Celsius, and trees to lose their leaves in the fall and grow leaves of the same kind the next spring. We expect ourselves to wake up in the same bed in which we went to sleep the night before, and to be much the same as we were the night before—more rested, perhaps, but the same sex and size and age and weight and with the same skills and failings.

But why *should* you expect such things? Why should you be *surprised* if, like Gregor Samsa in Kafka's *Metamorphosis,* you awoke one morning to discover that you had become a giant cockroach? What makes that any less likely than waking up to discover yourself much the same as you were the preceding night?

Such questions form the starting point for a full-fledged philosophical dialectic. One initial response to them is likely to be something like this: The fact is that people just *don't* go to bed as humans and wake up as cockroaches. If sometimes they did and sometimes they didn't, then I'd admit that when I went to bed at night I wouldn't know what to expect the next morning. But, in fact, I go to bed each night expecting to wake up much the same in the morning, and I *do* wake up much the same in the morning. What makes it *reasonable* for me to expect to do so, then, is that this expectation invariably proves correct. And this is true in general. What shows our expectations about the future to be reasonable is the fact that they work. Our expectations are regularly confirmed by experience. What could be more reasonable than that?

Such a response, however, is open to the charge of question begging. Here, with a slightly different emphasis, is how Bertrand Russell once formulated that charge:

> It has been argued that we have reason to know that the future will resemble the past, because what was the future has constantly become the past, so that we really have experience of the future, namely of times which were formerly future, which we may call past futures. But such an argument really begs the very question at issue. We have experience of past futures, but not of future futures, and the question is: Will future futures resemble past futures? This question is not to be answered by an argument which starts from past futures alone.[3]

In the initial response that we've been considering, the claim is that our expectations about the future are shown to be reasonable by the fact that they work, that they are regularly confirmed by experience. But are they? Well, we might concede that they so far always *have been*. But will they continue to be? We certainly *expect* them to be, of course, but that is an expectation about the future. The response simply assumes that it is a *reasonable* expectation. The issue in dispute, however, is whether *any* expectations about the future are reasonable. And so the response begs the question.

Instead of Russell's "past futures" and "future futures," we have here our past expectations and our future expectations. But the critical point is the same. The question is whether any of our expectations are reasonable. The response points out that any expectation that works is reasonable and that our past expectations have worked. Will our future expectations also work? We can't say for sure, of course, but the response takes it for granted that it is, in any case, *reasonable to expect* our future expectations to work. But that is precisely supposing that at least one expectation is reasonable. An argument which uses *that* premise to reach the conclusion that some expectations are reasonable thus uses its own conclusion as a premise, and thereby violates the canons of rational practice. Our responder is guilty of begging the question. And that is a second way to criticize a philosopher.

3.   *Infinite Regress*

Beginning students in philosophy—and even some more advanced ones—are often rather intimidated by the word 'infinite'. They tend to think of Infinity as a *big*

---

[3]   Bertrand Russell, *The Problems of Philosophy* (New York: Oxford University Press; 1959), pp. 64–5.

thing, big enough to deserve a capital letter—so big, in fact, that people can't quite wrap their minds around it. "The Infinite is beyond human comprehension" is how the story goes.

Well, the pleasant truth of the matter is that there isn't a *thing* called "Infinity" or "the Infinite," with or without capital letters. (Of course, some philosopher might introduce such a peculiar thing into his world view—and he would then owe us an account of what he was talking about. But that comes later.) The word that does the conceptual work is not the noun 'infinity' or '*the* infinite', but rather the *adjective* 'infinite'. Infinity is not a thing—but there are infinite things. This may still sound a bit mysterious and intimidating, so let me remind you of one of them that's an old friend of yours.

The series of positive integers

$$1, 2, 3, 4, 5, \ldots$$

is a familiar example of an *infinite sequence*. In general, the sorts of things that are infinite are things like sequences, series, sets, classes, groups, and collections—things that are composed of a plurality of elements or members. Whether or not such a thing is infinite depends upon *how many* members it has. The series of positive integers has an infinite number of members.[4] Infinity is not, as it were, a "super number" *in* the sequence. It's a number *describing* the sequence, a commentary on how many members it contains.

The sequence of positive integers has no highest (last) member. As we progress along the sequence, we never reach an ending point—not because it is "too far away" but simply because there *isn't* any. Analogously, the sequence of negative integers has no first (lowest) member:

$$\ldots, -5, -4, -3, -2, -1$$

As we *regress* (travel back) along the sequence, we never reach a beginning point—again, not because it is "too far away" but simply because there isn't any. Some infinite collections, of course, aren't *ordered*, as the integers are. But from such an unordered set or collection of elements, there will always be an infinite number of ways to select elements one by one—$e_1, e_2, e_3, \ldots$—and *put* them in a sequence that matches up with, for instance, the integers:

$$1, 2, 3, 4, 5, \ldots$$

$$e_1, e_2, e_3, e_4, e_5, \ldots$$

What unifies these diverse examples of infinite things is the notion of a *non-terminating process*—a procedure for progressing or regressing along a sequence or for

---

[4] More precisely, it has a *denumerably* or *countably* infinite number of members. Not all infinite collections are the "same size," a puzzling claim that is explored and made quite precise in a branch of mathematics called "transfinite arithmetic."

selecting elements from an unordered collection that does not come to an end. At each step there is a rule for taking the next step, but there is no rule for stopping. Non-terminating processes can crop up in various places. Perpetual check in chess is an example of such a process. (A special stopping rule had to be added to the rules of chess in order to guarantee that every game would necessarily sooner or later come to an end.)

The sort of infinite regress of interest to philosophers involves a non-terminating *rational* process—a process of drawing conclusions, giving reasons, explaining, justifying, deriving, and so on. Now there is nothing wrong with non-terminating rational processes in general. Suppose, for example, that Tom is tall. Then it is perfectly possible to derive, step by step, an infinite number of (completely uninteresting) consequences from this supposition. Let '(1)' abbreviate 'Tom is tall'. Then, from (1), it follows that

	(2)	It is true that (1).
and	(3)	It is true that (2).
and	(4)	It is true that (3).

and so on without end (*ad infinitum* or "to infinity," as the Latin has it). All of these consequences are terribly dull, of course, but mere tediousness carries no philosophical weight, either for or against an argument.

In order for the discovery of a non-terminating rational process to bear *critically* on a philosophical view or thesis, some additional conditions must obtain. To begin with, the process in question must be a *regress*; it must dictate that some further step must always have been taken *before* any given step can be taken. Second, the proposed regress must be a genuine consequence of the philosophical view or thesis being criticized. Third, and even more important, there must be something *wrong* about the infinite process at issue. Its existence must constitute an incoherence in the overall philosophical position from which it has been derived. Here's a comparatively simple example, drawn from philosophical reflection on moral agency.

One traditional and plausible view concerning moral responsibility is that a person can justifiably be held accountable only for those actions that are in his or her control. If my behavior results from drugs or hypnosis, bodily manipulation by implanted electrodes or a team of hefty wrestlers, or a knee-jerk kind of reflex, neither praise nor blame attaches to it. Only what one does *voluntarily*, only one's voluntary acts, are legitimately open for moral appraisal. And so the questions naturally arise: Which acts are *voluntary* acts? In what does the voluntariness of an act consist? What *makes* a bit of behavior a voluntary act?

One classical answer to these questions, in turn, is that the voluntariness of an act consists in its having a special kind of *cause*. Responsibility attaches only to what one does "of one's own free will." A voluntary act, in other words, is one caused by a volition or *act of will*. What excuses my behavior in the cases listed above is that what I do is not something I *will* to do. My behavior in such circumstances is not caused by an act of my will but by chemical reactions or electrical discharges or the hypnotist's commands. Since I can be held morally accountable only for what I will to do, only for behavior which *does* result from acts of my will, in such cases I am off the hook.

Let us call this the Volitionist theory. The critical response to this theory begins by describing an infinite regress. Consider these acts of will themselves. Are they voluntary or involuntary? In order for the account of moral responsibility to have any plausibility at all, it seems, they must surely be voluntary. For suppose that they were not. Then an act of will would just be something that *happens* in me—like a chemical reaction or an electrical discharge—or something that happens *to* me—like a hypnotist's command. It would not be something in my control. Blaming *me* for my behavior under those circumstances would make no more sense than blaming a bullet for exploding when struck by the firing pin. The bullet had, so to speak, no choice in the matter. Something happened to it that caused it to explode. Similarly, if my acts of will were themselves involuntary, something that caused me to behave in this or that particular fashion would from time to time happen to me. But *I* would have no choice in the matter; it wouldn't be *my* fault.

So the Volitionist theory can supply an adequate account of the limits of moral responsibility only if the acts of will that it proposes as causes of the relevant behavior are themselves be voluntary. And in what will the voluntariness of an *act of will* consist? Why, in its having a special kind of cause, of course. According to the Volitionist theory, that's what makes *any* act voluntary. An act of will is voluntary just in case it is caused by a volition, that is, by *another* act of will.

And now we can see where the infinite regress comes in. The same question—voluntary or involuntary?—arises for these news acts of will, and, for the same reasons, it must receive the same answer. Each of them must be preceded by yet another act of will. It is a consequence of the Volitionist theory, then, that any voluntary act must be preceded by an *infinite series* of acts of will, each causing the act that follows it.

This discovery reveals an incoherence in the Volitionist theory. The theory holds, you will recall, that the voluntariness of any voluntary act consists in its being caused by an act of will. But what our most recent reasoning makes clear is that not just any act of will is good enough. It must, in fact, be a *voluntary* act of will. And if this is so, we haven't been given an answer to our original question. We can only understand *this* answer if we already know what makes an act of will voluntary. But our original question was: What makes *any* act voluntary? The only course open to us at this point is to apply the Volitionist theory again—but when we do so, all we discover is that we need to posit yet another *voluntary* act of will. The original question—what makes *any* act voluntary?—does not go away.

That is the essence of this mode of criticism. The question does not go away. That is what makes this challenge dialectical rather than logical. Infinite regress disqualifies a proposed answer *as an answer*, for something qualifies as an answer to a question only if one can understand it without already knowing the answer to the question. That is the canon of rational practice violated by a philosopher who offers such an answer. He commits himself to what is known in the trade as a *vicious* infinite regress. (An infinite regress that is not vicious, in contrast, is called *benign*.)

In outline, this is the strategy of our third way to criticize a philosopher. The Volitionist theory of the voluntariness of voluntary acts fails, on this account, by having among its consequences a vicious infinite regress. It is an infinite *regress* because the voluntariness of an act will be secured only if the voluntariness of its volitional cause is *already* secured. If the cause itself is what is to guarantee the voluntariness of the effect, the voluntariness of the cause must be accounted for *before* the voluntariness of the effect. And it is a *vicious* regress because, given that the hypothesized volitional cause is itself an act (an act of will), the *problem* of supplying an account of its voluntariness is identical to the problem with which our inquiry began, the problem of accounting for the voluntariness of *any* voluntary act. The Volitionist proposal thereby violates a canon of rational practice. It disqualifies itself as an answer to our original question, for something qualifies as such an answer only if one can understand it without already knowing the answer to the question.

Only an infinite regress that exhibits this sort of dialectical incoherence in a philosophical view is properly regarded as a *vicious* regress, and only the discovery of such a genuinely vicious regress carries indisputable critical weight. Determining whether a particular infinite regress is vicious or benign, however, is a problem of the same delicacy and complexity as determining whether a given argument is or is not question begging. As with question begging, the dialectical environment of an infinite regress is crucial. The same thesis can imply a benign regress in one setting, a vicious regress in another, and no regress at all in yet another. For these reasons, authentic cases of vicious infinite regress are relatively rare in philosophical practice—rarer, in fact, than many practicing philosophers think. Yet, as with genuinely question-begging arguments, sometimes the dialectical context is just right and an explanatory hypothesis is proposed that does imply a truly vicious regress. If you can discover and exhibit such a case, then you will indeed have mastered a third way to criticize a philosopher.

4. Lost Contrast

"Equality before the law" is a maxim that applies to the laws of logic more surely than to the laws of our imperfect society. As a positive principle, it requires that similar cases receive similar treatment. As a negative principle, it instructs us that unlike treatment of cases can be justified only if we can point to features exhibited by one case but not by the other. There is to be no discrimination unless there is a difference.

Applied to reasoning, the principle gives us yet another family of canons of rational practice. In the case of arguments, it instructs us that like premises support like conclusions. Regarding rational inquiry in general, it tells us that similar data confirm similar hypotheses and that analogous phenomena should receive analogous explanations. The underlying point of all these canons is this: The relations of support or implication between premises and conclusion, of explanation between theory and phenomenon, and of confirmation between data and hypothesis are all, in the broadest sense, logical relations—and logic is *formal*. The obtaining of logical relations is a matter of abstract patterns of reasoning and evidence rather than a matter of specific content. The similarities, likenesses, and analogies mentioned in these canons, then, are basically formal similarities. They concern the general pattern of premises, data, or phenomena without being overly worried about what those claims might say in detail.

Philosophers draw distinctions. The dialectical character of philosophical methodology regularly gives rise to *dichotomies*—"either-or" divisions marked by pairs of concepts that are intended to *contrast* with one another and stand in opposition. We have already played with a few of these and mentioned a few others—

necessary *vs.* contingent, free *vs.* determined, mental *vs.* material. One useful item to have in our critical toolbox, then, would be an instrument with which one could assess such distinctions or, more precisely, evaluate the reasoning by which some philosopher attempts to introduce and support some such dichotomy.

Our maxim of equality and the canons of rational practice to which it points are just such tools. Every distinction requires a difference. If, however, there is no difference, then the supposed distinction evaporates; the intended contrast is *lost*. What we need to do, therefore, is to examine the sorts of considerations that a philosopher cites in favor of setting particular items on one side or the other of a proposed dichotomy. Suppose, for example, that a philosopher is trying to sort X's from Y's. Let us say that she classifies A as an X and B as a Y. Our maxim of equality tells us that this classification will be legitimate only if she can point to a *relevant difference* between A and B. If, on the other hand, for every consideration that favors classifying A as an X, we can find a parallel consideration applying to B; and if, for every consideration that favors classifying B as a Y, we can find a parallel consideration applying to A—if, in short, we can show that there is no relevant difference between A and B—then the intended contrast is lost. A and B may both be X's or they may both be Y's, or for that matter, neither may be either an X or a Y; but if there is no relevant difference between A and B, we may at least be sure that there can be no legitimate distinction in their classification. And now it's time for an example.

Perhaps the supreme master of this style of criticism was Bishop George Berkeley. The main distinction that Berkeley attempted to run to ground was that between *mind* and *matter*. There is nothing, he proposed to show, that has an absolute existence outside the mind. The *esse* of the world is *percipi*—the existence of the world consists in its being perceived. (On the face of it, this is a completely outrageous thesis—but not when Berkeley gets finished with it!) To this end, Berkeley wrote for us three of the most charming dialogues in philosophy, the dialogues between Hylas (from the Greek word *hyle*, meaning "matter") and Philonous (from *philos nous,* the "lover of mind"). These dialogues are gems of dialectic. Philonous inexorably presses the critical attack against a tenacious Hylas, who retreats slowly from formulation to reformulation, always holding fast to his root conviction that matter is *real*.

The question with which the first of Berkeley's three dialogues opens is whether *sensible qualities* exist outside the mind. By 'sensible qualities', Berkeley means those properties of objects accessible to the various senses—colors, shapes, sounds, flavors, odors, textures, and heat and cold. Hylas, of course, answers yes. Sensible qualities are "out there" in the world, in contrast, for example, to *pains*, which are merely "in us" and do not exist at all unless they are experienced (felt) by someone. Using the example of heat, Berkeley—speaking through Philonous—proceeds to criticize Hylas's distinction. He does so on the grounds of lost contrast:

PHILONOUS: Tell me whether, in two cases exactly alike, we ought
                      not to make the same judgment?

HYLAS: We ought.

PHILONOUS: When a pin pricks your finger, does it not rend and divide the fibers of your flesh?

HYLAS: It does.

PHILONOUS: And when a coal burns your finger, does it any more?

HYLAS: It does not.

PHILONOUS: Since, therefore, you neither judge the sensation itself occasioned by the pin, nor anything like it to be in the pin, you should not, conformably to what you have now granted, judge the sensation occasioned by the fire, or anything like it, to be in the fire.[5]

Hylas would classify sensations of heat as "in the fire" but sensations of pain as "in us." Philonous replies that this is a distinction without a difference. Is the heat to be located in the fire because we feel it whenever the fire acts on us? Then the pain belongs in the pin, for we feel it whenever the pin pricks us. Is the pain to be located in us because it is a sensation that we feel? Then the heat is in us too, for it is also a sensation that we feel. For every consideration in favor of classifying the heat as located "in the fire" there is a parallel consideration applying to the pain, and for every consideration in favor of classifying the pain as located "in us," we can find a similar consideration applying to the heat. There is no relevant difference. The intended contrast is lost. Heat and pain may *both* be "out there" or they may *both* be "in us." This argument cannot, by itself, tell us which of these conclusions finally to endorse. But we can be sure of at least this much: There can be no distinction in their classification; both heat and pain must be classified in the *same* way. A philosopher who, like Hylas, proposes unequal treatment for heat and pain without citing a relevant difference violates a canon of rational practice. His supposed distinction rests on a lost contrast. And that is a fourth way to criticize a philosopher.

5.   *Emptiness*

There is, I assure you, a demon in my wristwatch. How interesting, you might say. Let us open up the watch and have a look at it. You may open the watch if you wish, I reply, but it will avail you little. I neglected to mention a salient fact: It is an *invisible* demon. Let me feel it then, you say. Sorry, I answer, it's also an *intangible* demon. Can I hear it? you ask. No, it's *inaudible*—and *odorless* and *tasteless*, too, if it comes to that. Well then, you quite reasonably ask, how do you know it's there? Is it radioactive? No. Magnetic? No. Can you pick up its emanations on CB radio? No. Well, then, you ask, does it at least affect the workings of the watch? Does the watch run slower or faster, for example, on account of the demon in it? I can save you a lot of trouble, I reply. It doesn't affect the workings of the watch at all. It is, in fact, a *wholly undetectable* demon. But nevertheless, I assure you that there is a demon in my wristwatch.

---

[5]   George Berkeley, *Three Dialogues Between Hylas and Philonous* (Indianapolis and New York: Bobbs-Merrill; 1954), p. 18.

And now, if you have your wits about you, what you say next is something like this: Tell me, what is the difference between a wristwatch containing a wholly undetectable demon and a wristwatch containing *no demon at all?*[6]

What shall we say about my claim "There is a demon in my wristwatch" in these circumstances? Is it *true?* Well, suppose we said it is. What would follow from that? It doesn't follow that anyone at any time in any situation will see or hear or smell or taste or feel anything in particular. It doesn't follow that a Geiger counter, or a CB radio, or even the watch itself, or anything else, for that matter, will ever behave in any special way. Evidently, in fact, nothing significant follows from it at all.

Well then, shall we say that the claim is *false,* that there *isn't* a demon in my wristwatch? And what would follow from that? Just what would we be *denying?* What would we be ruling out? Why, exactly the same thing, of course—namely, nothing at all. So it really doesn't make any difference what we say, does it?

At the beginning, it looked as if I were making a straightforward, although startling, claim about my wristwatch, rather like "There is a gear in my wristwatch" or "There is a mainspring in my wristwatch." (Both of which happen to be false, by the way; I have a solid-state digital LCD watch.) But now it turns out that I might as well have said "There is a mulpsible in my wristwatch" and, when asked what a mulpsible *is,* replied, "I haven't the foggiest idea."

For that matter, just what does my wristwatch have to do with what I said? If I had said "There is a gear ..." or "There is a mainspring ...", then, by going on to say "in my wristwatch," I would have told you *where to look* if you were interested in finding out whether what I said was true or false. But what's going on in my wristwatch has turned out to be completely *irrelevant* to the question of whether what I said, "There is a demon in my wristwatch," is true or false. *Everything* turned out to be completely irrelevant to that question. You might as well look at my teacup or at your own left shoe. Nothing you detected there would have any more bearing on the truth or falsehood of what I said than what you could detect in my wristwatch. In an important sense, then, it seems that my claim wasn't really *about* my wristwatch at all. The *words* were there, all right, but for all the help they gave you in understanding what I was saying, they could just as well have been replaced by any other words.

For that matter, couldn't they just as well have been replaced by no words at all? I might as well have said, "Astogobble mixplet is krand sumdickel." And would that be true or false? Why, it isn't even a *candidate.* It isn't even in the true-or-false line of work!

The surprising discovery is that my original claim, "There is a demon in my wristwatch"—although it *looked* quite different (and perhaps filled your imagination with many charming pictures)—turned out to be in the same boat. There's no reason to say that it's true, and there's no reason to say that it's false either. The best thing to say about it is that it turns out not to be in that line of work at all. It turns out to be *empty.*

This is lost contrast, but with a vengeance—lost contrast carried to its final extreme. It isn't as if there were a perfectly good distinction between ordinary wrist-

---

[6] This example is inspired by John Wisdom's "parable of the gardener" in Essay X of *Logic and Language,* First Series, ed. Antony Flew (Oxford: Basil Blackwell, 1960).

watches and wristwatches inhabited by undetectable demons, the only problem being whether *your* watch and *my* watch should be classified in the same way. We are worse off here than that. It's not that a distinction is being misapplied or applied groundlessly. Rather, no distinction has been put on the table in the first place. The sentence "There is a demon in my wristwatch" hasn't been given any job to do. It has nothing to do with demons or with wristwatches or with anything else. It's just something I *say* from time to time, a noise that I make, like a grunt or a whistle—but it's empty. A contrast has been lost, all right, but it's not the contrast between two sorts of wristwatches; it's the contrast between *saying something true or false* and *just making noise*.

There's a canon of rational practice at stake here. One way to put it is this: Good grammar does not a thesis make. Meaningful claims must have meaningful consequences. Conversely, if, as the dialectic proceeds, a claim becomes progressively disconnected from all positive consequences, it loses its original *prima facie* credentials as a *thesis* to be defended or criticized. To defend a claim is to argue for its truth; to criticize it is to produce reasons for its advocate to abandon it as false. Either procedure makes sense, however, only if it is presupposed that the claim is in the true-or-false line of work to begin with, that it is a claim with a content. For the acceptance or rejection of a given thesis, you will recall, depends ultimately on whether it can successfully be shown to cohere or conflict with a large family of claims characteristic of a dialectical philosophical position. If a claim is totally disconnected from any positive consequences, however, it can *neither* cohere *nor* conflict with any other claims. Such a claim, then, is neither defensible nor criticizable. It is not, therefore, a debatable *thesis* at all. It is empty.

And how does all this look in practice? A few pages ago, we met Hylas near the beginning of Berkeley's three dialogues. Look at him now, fighting and dying in the last ditch for the reality of matter:

PHILONOUS:	… please … inform me after what manner you suppose [matter] to exist, or what you mean by its "existence"?
HYLAS:	It neither thinks nor acts, neither perceives nor is perceived.
PHILONOUS:	But what is there positive in your abstracted notion of its existence?
HYLAS:	Upon a nice observation, I do not find I have any positive notion or meaning at all. I tell you again, I am not ashamed to own my ignorance. I know not what is meant by its existence or how it exists.

Philonous moves in for the kill:

PHILONOUS:	When, therefore, you speak of the existence of matter, you have not any notion in your mind?
HYLAS:	None at all.

PHILONOUS: Pray tell me if the case stands not thus: at first, from a belief of material substance, you would have it that the immediate objects existed without the mind; then, that they are archetypes; then, causes; next, instruments; then, occasions; lastly, *something in general*, which being interpreted proves *nothing*. So matter comes to nothing. What think you, Hylas, is not this a fair summary of your whole proceeding?

HYLAS: Be that as it will, yet I still insist upon it, that our not being able to conceive a thing is no guarantee against its existence.

PHILONOUS: That from a cause, effect, operation, sign, or other circumstance there may reasonably be inferred the existence of a thing not immediately perceived; and that it were absurd for any man to argue against the existence of that thing, from his having no direct and positive notion of it, I freely own. But where there is nothing of all this, where neither reason nor revelation induces us to believe the existence of a thing, where we have not even a relative notion of it, where an abstraction is made from perceiving and being perceived, from spirit and idea, lastly, where there is not so much as the most inadequate or faint idea pretended to, I will not, indeed, thence conclude against the reality of any notion or existence of anything; but my inference shall be that you mean nothing at all, that you employ words to no manner of purpose, without any design or signification whatsoever. And I leave it to you to consider how mere jargon should be treated.[7]

What Philonous is saying to Hylas (and thus what Berkeley is in effect saying to his philosophical predecessor John Locke, who had advocated the reality of matter) is this: Your claim "Matter exists" is empty. By progressively insulating it from any positive consequences, you have rendered your claim devoid of any content and reduced it to mere noise. And, in so doing, you have opted out of the dialectical game. I am relieved of my philosophical obligation to demonstrate an incoherence arising from your thesis for the simple reason that you are no longer advancing a thesis. "Where there are no ideas, there no repugnancy can be demonstrated between ideas." You have violated what may be the most fundamental canon of rational practice of them all, the basic presupposition of any method of rational inquiry—namely, that there *be* a thesis about which to inquire. And so this round of the game is over. Mind triumphs over matter, so to speak—but it wins by a forfeit.

And that, at last, is our fifth way to criticize a philosopher.

---

[7] Berkeley, *Three Dialogues Between Hylas and Philonous,* pp. 67–8.

CHAPTER EIGHT

Definitions, Analogies, and Thought Experiments

O ur judgment regarding the success or failure of a piece of philosophical reasoning is likely to hinge on how we interpret or construe certain *terms* that
play important roles within the dialectical proceedings. Some of these
terms—such as 'analytic', 'synthetic', 'a priori', 'a posteriori', 'counterfactual', 'substance', 'attribute', 'particular', and 'sense datum'—are bits of technical jargon, terms
that philosophers have invented or borrowed to signal certain ideas or mark certain
distinctions that are less clearly delineated, or even not explicitly acknowledged at all,
by our everyday vocabulary. Sometimes, however, they will be terms drawn from that
everyday vocabulary—'certainty', 'necessity', 'idea', 'concept', 'sensation', 'rights',
and 'values', for example—which some philosopher is using in an especially restricted or obviously unusual way in the service of his or her wider project. In any event,
our judgment regarding whether what a philosopher says is *true* will characteristically
turn on our understanding of what that philosopher *means* by what he or she has
said—and so it will be useful briefly to explore how you might go about *finding out*
(or deciding) just what it is that some philosopher means by this or that term.

It is also worth noting that philosophers, alas, are not always so helpful as to present their views and reasonings in the form of direct arguments, needing only a bit of
"tidying up" in order to identify their patterns, premises, and presuppositions. Any
philosophical work is also, among other things, a *literary* entity, and its style can range
from the dry formalism of a legal brief to charming dialogues of the sort that we've
lately been examining. In addition to both direct and dialectical *argument*, then, you
are likely to encounter in philosophical writings a rich set of *rhetorical* strategies—
that is, strategies aimed not so much at demonstrating a conclusion by logically deriving it from agreeable premises but at rendering a conclusion *plausible* by showing that
it hangs together with other, well-understood ways of thinking about the world, or that
it could account for something which otherwise would remain puzzling and obscure.
While there is, of course, no way to enumerate and examine all possible such rhetorical strategies, several of them are sufficiently popular and fruitful to deserve being
mentioned in an introductory handbook such as this.

These, then, will be the themes of the present chapter. I shall first say a few cautionary words about *meanings*—and, in particular, about dictionaries and
"definitions"; and then discuss a pair of useful rhetorical strategies that are especially

characteristic of philosophical writings—the use of *analogies* and the imaginative appeal to *thought experiments*.

What Your Dictionary Can't Tell You

When you are puzzled by an unfamiliar word, the usual thing to do is reach for the nearest dictionary, and what you find there is indeed often helpful. That is, what you find in a dictionary often serves to remove your initial puzzlement and to enable you to grasp what some author is driving at and get on with your reading. One common way of describing this sort of occurrence is in terms of "meanings." Initially, you are puzzled about "what the *author* means" because you don't understand "what some *word* means." So you "look up the meaning of the word" in your dictionary, and, afterward, you know both "what the word means" and "what the author means." Your puzzlement was a puzzlement about "meanings" and your appeal to the dictionary resolved that puzzlement. It is only natural, then, to suppose that what one finds in a dictionary *are* "the meanings of words"—that is, to suppose that a dictionary *contains meanings*. It is only natural—but it is also a mistake.

What one finds in a dictionary are not "the meanings of words"; what one finds are only *more words*. That, indeed, is the first rule of dictionary-making: Every word must have an *entry*, and every entry will consist of *other words*. A second rule is part of what makes the dictionary so helpful in cases like the one I've been describing: When the entry word is *unfamiliar* (rarely or infrequently used), the other words should be *more familiar* (commonly and frequently used). It would be a poor dictionary indeed which "defined" the entry word 'persiflage' by offering 'badinage', when 'banter' and 'good-humored teasing and joking' are ever so much more helpful.

Now *sometimes* it will, in fact, turn out that the other words following an entry word collectively do about the same job in speech and writing that the entry word itself does. Sometimes, that is, it would usually be in order to *replace* the entry word with the other words. Doing so would not materially distort the sense of the original text. In such a case we can indeed speak of the dictionary entry as a "definition" and say that the other words are (roughly) *synonymous* with the entry word, that they "have (approximately) the same meaning." But it would be a mistake to conclude on that account that the dictionary "contains" or even "gives" meanings. What a dictionary contains is *more words*, and it "gives meanings" only in the sense that those other words are sometimes familiar and well-understood possible *substitutes* for the unfamiliar and puzzling entry words that they accompany.

Sometimes, however, the words standing alongside an entry word are not words that could *do* roughly the same job in speech and writing as the entry itself. Sometimes, for instance, they are words that *describe* that job or give *examples* of the entry word in action:

> **not:** used to express negation, denial, refusal, or prohibition: *It's not far from here. You must not do that.*

And sometimes the relationship between the other words and the entry word is fairly complicated. The entry

green: the color of growing foliage, between yellow and blue
                       in the spectrum,

for instance, gives a pair of *recipes* for locating a *sample* of the color green: Look at some growing foliage, or look between yellow and blue in the spectrum. (Of course, you had better look at some *green* foliage. Some plants have *red* foliage, for example, and they'd be no help at all. And, by the way, do make sure that you've got a *complete* spectrum—and that you're looking at it in normal conditions and not, for instance, through a piece of colored glass.)

Editors of dictionaries arrive at their decisions regarding what to put next to an entry word in two ways. If the entry word is a common one, in widespread everyday use, they extract a large set of *samples* from novels, magazines, newspapers, transcripts of radio and television broadcasts, and other contexts in which the word appears. They then attempt to diagnose from these samples the way or ways in which the word is *generally* used—the job or jobs it is usually doing in speech or writing— and to supply other words that either *do* roughly the same job, or *describe* that job, or are related to the entry word in some other potentially useful way (as in the example of 'green'). If, on the other hand, the entry word is unusual, rare, or technical— belonging, for instance, to the specialized vocabulary of medicine or biology or engineering or law … or philosophy—it will not be possible to assemble such a broad sampling of its uses. In such a case, the lexicographer characteristically relies upon a panel of *consultants* who are themselves academic *specialists*—physicians, biologists, engineers, lawyers … or philosophers—seeking, and typically accepting, *their* recommendations of other words to put alongside the unfamiliar entry word.

What follows from these facts of life, we can conclude, is that a dictionary is not a suitable place to look for help if your puzzlement about a word is a *philosophical* puzzlement, that is, a puzzlement about the particular way in which some individual philosopher is using that word in a piece of reasoning that you are attempting to evaluate. If the term in question is a *familiar* one—for example, 'idea' or 'sensation'— that is being used by the philosopher in some limited, novel, creative, or unfamiliar way in service of his or her specific dialectical ends, then the dictionary's reconstruction of the usual and customary job done by that term in speech and writing is not likely to prove particularly helpful to you. But if the word in question is a *purely* technical term—for example, 'apperception' or 'epiphenomenon'—then, if a dictionary contains any entry for the word at all, what it will have to offer you at best is characteristically only *another philosopher's conclusion* about what the first philosopher, the one you are reading, was up to; and that conclusion will inevitably be colored by the consultant's own philosophical views and characteristic vocabulary. In neither case, alas, will your dictionary give you "*the* meaning" of the troublesome term, much less "the *true* meaning."

Suppose, for instance, that you are reading Aristotle's *Metaphysics* and you become puzzled by the way in which he is using the terms (translated as) 'form' and 'matter'. You are not clear about "what Aristotle meant" by those words. So you consult a dictionary—let us even say a *special* dictionary, devoted exclusively to philosophical terminology—and there you find entries for 'form' and 'matter' ostensibly describing, among other things, how Aristotle used those terms in his *Metaphysics*.

Some other philosopher, serving as a consultant specialist, has written entries for those terms purporting to explain "what Aristotle meant" by those terms. But how did that consultant specialist arrive at *her* individual notion of what Aristotle meant by 'form' and 'matter' in the *Metaphysics?* Not, you can be sure, by looking up 'form' and 'matter' in yet another dictionary, but, obviously, by *studying* Aristotle's work and trying to puzzle out what Aristotle *meant* there by 'form' and 'matter' from what Aristotle there *said* about form and matter. But that's precisely what *you* were in the process of doing when you reached for the dictionary in the first place. And that, of course, is what you will *still* need to do in such a case; for, in the end, it remains your responsibility to judge whether or not such a consultant philosopher has understood Aristotle *correctly*.

At best, then, the entries in such a dictionary may serve to equip you with a *provisional* interpretation of some problematic terminology. Since, however, dictionaries contain only humanly formulated words and not divinely inspired meanings, any such interpretation will at most be a point from which to begin. It will still remain for you to *test* that interpretation against the text itself—that is, to judge whether the philosopher's arguments indeed make sense when his or her vocabulary is understood in the suggested way and then, if they do, to judge whether, on this or that interpretation, they turn out to be cogent and compelling arguments.

A dictionary is indisputably useful—you should certainly own a good one—but it cannot substitute for the hard work of philosophical thinking. For a dictionary can tell you neither what a word "*really* means" nor what some specific philosopher meant *by* that word (that is, how he or she was individually using it) on some particular dialectical occasion. It cannot tell you the former, the "real" or "true" meaning of the word, for there exists no such mythical beast to be hunted down. And it has no *special* authority with regard to the latter, a specific philosopher's particular usages, for, in the end, dictionary-makers have nothing to go on but what you yourself have to go on: the writings of that philosopher himself, and the fallible judgment of one or more human beings about how those writings are best and properly to be understood.

Dialectical Likenesses

If someone finds it difficult to understand the structure of a hydrogen atom, it may be helpful to compare it to the structure of the solar system—the massive proton nucleus standing at the center like a sun, orbited by a comparatively less massive "planetary" electron. If an anthropologist finds it difficult to describe the role of certain magical rituals in a primitive culture, she may find it useful to draw parallels between those rituals and certain religious rites found within her own culture. Analogical thinking, in other words, is a common tool for furthering understanding and communication in the physical and social sciences—and so too in philosophy. And this fact immediately makes it appropriate to sound a cautionary note: Not everything that a philosopher says in the course of expounding and defending his or her point of view is intended to be (or should be) taken *literally*.

Sometimes, of course, a philosopher is quite explicit about his or her analogical intentions. In his *Republic,* for example, Plato turns from an investigation of the question "What constitutes a just *person?*"—that is, "What is the nature of this desirable trait of character, justice, in a virtuous individual?"—to consider the question "What constitutes a just *civil society?*"—that is, "What is the nature of this desirable condition, justice, in the Greek *polis* (city-state)?" His reason, he tells us, is that the *polis* is "the soul writ large." Not, of course, that the city-state *is* a giant soul, or the human soul a miniature city-state, but that there are important *analogies*—dialectical likenesses—between an individual soul and a political community, likenesses that can be exploited in a philosophical exploration of what contributes to the moral character of a virtuous person.

The use of such explicit analogies is a perennial feature of philosophical thinking. We find it, for instance, in Locke's description of the human mind as a *tabula rasa,* a "blank tablet" upon which "experience writes its record." We find it in Rousseau's likening the grounding of civil society to the signing of a "social contract" according to which each participant agrees to surrender certain individual freedoms in the interest of securing a greater collective good. And we find it today, for example, in Thomas Kuhn's characterization of major theory changes in the physical sciences as "revolutions," and in the comparison of human cognitive processes to the operations of a digital computer—a comparison that has become a commonplace of contemporary philosophy of mind. In each instance, the explicit intent is not to *identify* the one thing with the other, but rather to stress certain *similarities* of one to the other. Acknowledging such similarities, in turn, is then seen as carrying with it a commitment to accepting significant *philosophical* theses about the subjects of such analogical comparisons: for instance, that there is no "innate knowledge"; that the surrender of individual rights in a political community is not coercive; that "scientific progress" is partially determined by "irrational" sociocultural factors; or that we need introduce no special "nonphysical" entities (a mind or a soul) to explain our own cognitive capabilities.

But analogical thinking also often plays a more subtle role in philosophical theorizing. Sometimes a particular dialectical similarity is not explicitly formulated in the interest of securing the acceptance of a significant philosophical thesis, but is simply *taken for granted* in the *description* of some phenomenon which then serves as the point of departure for further philosophical discussions.

A philosopher engaged in offering a theory of sensations, for example, may proceed on the *assumption* that the sentence

(1)   Tom felt a sharp pain in his foot,

is to be understood by analogy to

(2)   Ellen saw a red cup on the table.

The ensuing discussion is then likely to take some odd turns, turns that in fact have been more or less "predetermined" by this tacit analogical presupposition. There will be worries about the "privacy" of pains. (Ellen and Eloise can obviously both see the *same* red cup. Can Tom and Timothy both feel the *same* sharp pain?) There will be worries about how one *counts* pains. (There's a difference between Ellen's seeing one red cup on two different occasions and her seeing two exactly similar red cups, a different one on each occasion. But is there a difference between Tom's feeling one sharp pain twice and his feeling two exactly similar sharp pains, a different one on each occasion?) And there will be worries about the *location* of pains. (If the table is in the kitchen, then when Ellen sees a cup on the table she sees a cup in the kitchen. But even if Tom's foot is in his shoe, when Tom feels a pain in his foot he does *not* feel a pain in his shoe. Why not?)

Whether an analogy be explicit or merely tacit, however, your approach to the critical appraisal of its cogency and pertinence remains the same. You need to ask, first, what *points* of analogy—precisely what similarities or likenesses—the philosopher is proposing to exploit in his or her theorizing; second, whether those similarities or likenesses in fact *obtain*; and, third, whether there are any significant points of *dis*-analogy that vitiate the force of the intended or presupposed comparison. And it will often be useful in such cases to attempt to come up with a comparison of your own, an *alternative* analogy, that highlights the *dis*-similarities between the two phenomena which the philosopher whose work you are evaluating has undertaken to assimilate to a single dialectical pattern.

You might, for example, challenge Rousseau's explicit analogy between civic duties and contractual obligations on the issue of *voluntariness*, arguing that contracting parties commit themselves deliberately and self-consciously, whereas one is simply *born into* some civil society or other. And you might take on the tacit analogy between feeling a pain and seeing a cup by suggesting that what appears to be the *point* of the analogy—that "feeling," like "seeing," is a *relation* between a person and something else, some separate "object"—does not in fact obtain. Instead of understanding sentence (1) on the model of sentence (2), for instance, we might try to understanding it by analogy with

(3)   Margaret wore a warm smile on her face,

and, noting that (3) is just a long-winded way of saying

(3*)   Margaret smiled warmly,

suggest that (1), rather than pointing to a relation between Tom and some "private object," is just a long-winded way of saying something like

(1*)   Tom's foot hurt sharply.

The Place of Science Fiction in Philosophy

The final feature of philosophical writing I want to address in this chapter is philosophers' frequent use of *thought experiments*—that is, their imaginative descriptions of situations that do not *in fact* obtain. Appeals to thought experiments of this sort serve a number of purposes in philosophical works. Indeed, we have already encountered some of them in our discussions of validity and invalidity.

You may remember, for instance, my dog Fido (who would have four legs and a tail if he were a cat, and who *does* have four legs and a tail, but is *not* a cat). Well, the fact of the matter is that I don't have a dog named Fido. I don't have any dog at all. The situation that I described in order to come up with some true premises ("If Fido is a cat, then he has four legs and a tail" and "Fido has four legs and a tail") and a false conclusion ("Fido is a cat") is a situation that does not in fact obtain. My counterexample was a thought experiment. But it got the job done all the same. For, since an argument's form is valid only if the truth of its premises *guarantees* the truth of its conclusion, all that we need do in order to demonstrate that an argument is invalid is to show that it is *possible* for another argument to have both the same form and true premises—but, for all that, a false conclusion.

This observation highlights what is in fact the characteristic role of such imaginative exercises in philosophical writing: The purpose of a thought experiment is to establish that something is *possible*. Now the main sort of possibility that's typically of interest to philosophers is not practical or technological possibility (whether, for instance, it is now realistically possible, either practically or technologically, to establish a colony on the moon), but rather what is usually called "logical possibility." A situation or state of affairs is *logically* possible just in case it can be described without logical absurdity, that is, without contradicting oneself. And philosophers are interested in logical possibility because figuring out whether some situation is logically possible is often a crucial step in determining whether *another* state of affairs is or is not *necessary,* or in arguing that some problematic philosophical thesis is or is not in fact *true.*

Law enforcement agencies, for instance, use fingerprints to determine the identity of persons in their custody. If the fingerprints of a captured suspect match the fingerprints of a wanted criminal, the police and the courts regularly conclude that the suspect in custody *is* the wanted criminal. A philosopher interested in the concept of personal identity, however, will point out that the principle "Sameness of fingerprints implies sameness of persons" is *not* a necessary truth. We can easily imagine and coherently describe a situation in which two persons are born with the same fingerprints or in which a clever surgeon perfects a technique for altering fingerprints. It is, in other words, *logically* possible for two persons to have identical fingerprints or for one person to have different fingerprints at different times (although, as far as I know, neither of these situations now *in fact* obtains).

Where such thought experiments become particularly interesting is where the philosophical thesis at issue is a significant one and the state of affairs imaginatively described is correlatively complicated. A philosopher may attempt to convince us, for instance, that minds and bodies are *separate* entities by inviting us to imagine "two people *exchanging* bodies."

Surely you've seen this one depicted on television. Two people—Jack and Jill, let us say—sit in chairs alongside an intricate electronic device. Metal helmets are lowered onto their heads. The infernal machine flashes and buzzes and hums and spits out sparks. Jack and Jill slump forward, unconscious. Finally, after a brief interval, the person who *looks* like Jack (call him Punch) stands up and claims to *be* Jill, and the person who *looks* like Jill (call her Judy) stands up and claims to *be* Jack. And what's more, Punch now speaks and acts the way Jill used to speak and act, and Judy now similarly behaves the way Jack used to behave. This thought experiment shows, our philosopher concludes, that it is *logically possible* for two people to exchange bodies. It follows that a person cannot be *identified* with a body, but must rather be a *mind*—something separate from any particular body that, at least in principle, admits of being *transferred* from one body to another.

The critical evaluation of a philosophical conclusion grounded in such a dramatic thought experiment is a matter of some complexity. The most important point to keep in mind, however, is that what is at issue does *not* turn on anyone's powers of *imagination*. A state of affairs is logically possible, you should recall, just in case it can be consistently *described*, that is, described without contradiction or logical absurdity. Of course we can successfully imagine *something* in the case of Jack and Jill. We can even depict it on television. What is crucial for our philosopher's conclusions, however, is how whatever we successfully imagine should correctly be *described*. What we need to look at, in other words, is not the dramatic picture that the philosopher's thought experiment paints but rather what the philosopher *says* (or simply takes for granted) about what he invites us to visualize.

In this case, it is clear enough *what* is being claimed. Our philosopher wants us to *say* that, after the operation of the machine, Punch *is* Jill and Judy *is* Jack. But now it becomes appropriate to ask: What criterion is being employed to *identify* Jack and Jill here? It's clear enough, for example, that fingerprints *aren't* being treated as such a criterion. But then, what is? How, in other words, is one supposed to *determine*, after the experiment, who's who?

Well, it has to be by considering Punch and Judy's *behavior*, doesn't it?—how they act and what they say about themselves. But now you can object that this only shows us who they *think* they are. A lunatic, for example, may *say* that he's Napoleon. He may even *act* like he's Napoleon. But that isn't sufficient to show that he *is* Napoleon. Similarly, you can continue, Punch's claims and behavior don't establish that he *is* Jill (although he says he is), and Judy's don't establish that she *is* Jack (although she says she is). You can criticize a philosopher's thought experiment, in other words, by arguing that his or her *description* of what he or she has visualized or imagined does not stand up under examination. In this instance, for example, the description "two persons exchanging bodies" arguably rests upon a false presupposition, namely, that a person's beliefs and behavior suffice to establish that person's identity.

You can also criticize such a thought experiment, then, by offering an *alternative description* of it. What we have imagined, you might propose, is not a machine for "putting Jack into Jill's body and Jill into Jack's body." What we have imagined is a machine for simultaneously inducing a particular kind of *insanity* (say, "acute delusionary personality psychosis") in two people—a machine that has driven both Jack and Jill mad, so that Jack now thinks he is Jill and Jill now thinks she is Jack.

Introducing such an alternative description can "defuse" a thought experiment by showing that the imaginative exercise, even with all the vivid pictures it evokes, does not *by itself* support the intended philosophical conclusion (e.g., about minds and bodies). It does so only if one *takes for granted* certain additional premises (e.g., about how to determine who's who)—premises that you can then engage *argumentatively* in a critical discussion like that of any other, less picturesque, bit of philosophical writing.

Second Intermission

We have once again reached a point at which we would do well to pause and consolidate our gains.

What I have been discussing for the last three chapters is one basic form of philosophical essay, the critical examination of a view. There are other forms, of course, and I don't intend to neglect them, but the critical examination of a view is, in an important sense, the *fundamental* form, for it defines the sort of test that *any* philosophical effort must ultimately pass. A philosophical critique, so to speak, sets the boundaries of the playing field and lays down the ground rules of the game. In light of the unavoidably systematic and dialectical nature of philosophical views, that is, the only measure that one can *ultimately* employ in evaluating the acceptability of any constructive *or critical* philosophical proposal—including your own!—is an exploration of its ability to *stand up* under just this sort of critical examination.

In these chapters we have spent considerable time probing the details of the notion of "internal incoherence" that lies at the heart of any dialectical critique. We have found that it ranges from the relatively straightforward, although rare, discovery of an explicit self-contradiction to the subtler, but correlatively more frequent, matter of violations of general "canons of rational practice." It is such violations that give rise to what are characteristically thought of as particularly "philosophical" criticisms, and we have illustrated and explored five such criticisms in substantial detail—equivocation, question begging, infinite regress, lost contrast, and emptiness. While these are by no means the *only* ways in which a piece of philosophical reasoning can subtly take a wrong turn, like our more straightforward "froggy" invalid argument patterns and slippery modifier muddles discussed in earlier chapters, they are common enough confusions that you should be on the lookout for them—in your reading *and* in your own writing—whenever an argument arrives at a conclusion that you have reason to suspect might not be entirely in order.

Extracting the argument for a philosophical text, as we have noted, occasionally demands considerable exegetical skill, for philosophical essays are also literary works in which unfamiliar words sometimes surface, familiar words sometimes take on unfamiliar jobs, and rhetorical devices are pressed into expository and argumentative service. While there is, in the end, no substitute for *practice* in mastering the art of coming to critical terms with a piece of philosophical writing, I have tried in the last chapter to supply a few tips, too, for dealing with questions of meaning when they arise in philosophical inquiry and for recognizing, appreciating, and even criticizing appeals to analogies and to thought experiments in the conduct of a philosophical case.

All this has doubtless been rather a sizable chunk of material to assimilate at one stretch. Indeed, you are not likely to manage its assimilation short of attempting to *put it to use* in writing your own critical examinations of some philosophers' arguments and views. Once you have managed it, however, you will possess all the rudiments, not only for understanding philosophical thinking as it is practiced by others, but also for the practical philosophical *exercise* of that understanding in your own thinking and writing. What we need to do next, then, is to explore some of the more elaborate discursive structures that can be developed from these strategic themes, that is, some of the still larger patterns of thought within which the critical examination of a view may *itself* be embedded. Let me, then, bring this second intermission to a close and raise the curtain on our next act, a discussion of some of the *other* species of philosophical essay that you are likely to encounter in your reading—or, ideally, be challenged yourself to produce in your own writing.

CHAPTER NINE

Philosophical Essays: Adjudication of a Dispute

T he most straightforward development of the critical examination of a view is the adjudicatory essay. Here the author acts as a third party to a philosophical dispute and attempts to arrive at a verdict that properly takes into account the strengths and weaknesses of the competing positions. Such an adjudicatory essay can usefully be viewed as having a six-part structure:

A. Formulation of the issue
B. Exposition of position 1
C. Evaluation of position 1
D. Exposition of position 2
E. Evaluation of position 2
F. Resolution

There is nothing sacred about this ordering of elements, however. You may sometimes find it more convenient to collect together first expository and then evaluative elements, proceeding in the sequence A-B-D-C-E-F, or to adopt an oscillatory "see-saw" strategy in the central portion of the essay, alternating between one position and the other until both have been explained and explored piecemeal. Let's consider each of these six elements of an adjudicatory essay in detail.

A. Formulating the issue in dispute often makes severe demands on a student's interpretive abilities. Superficial peculiarities of terminology or expository style sometimes conceal disagreements or obscure potential agreement between the disputants. A careful and thorough reading of both texts is usually necessary in order to determine, from contextual clues provided by the detailed development of the reasoning, whether key terms are in fact being used and understood in the same way by both parties. Again, in consequence of philosophy's dialectical methodology, the visible topics of discussion may be only indirectly related to the main underlying issue of contention. Recall that, although the war is being waged over some central thesis, individual battles may be fought at some distance, over supporting premises. One useful strategy is to formulate the issue as a question to which the disputing parties do or would give differing answers. The question should be framed in such a way that it can be used as a guide to reading the disputed texts. Each text is then considered in relation to the proposed question, as argumentatively working toward some particular answer to it.

B. and **D.**   The exposition of the two positions should be conducted through the medium of the issue under dispute as you have formulated it. That is, the expository task becomes that of setting out the structure of argumentation supporting each competing view on the disputed issue, in a way that makes it clear how the considerations offered by each disputant in support of his or her view bear on that issue. Frequently this requires that the student reconstruct a piece of reasoning, as it were, in reverse, so that the connections between the disputed issue which is the philosophical starting point and the several dialectical considerations that form the philosophical talking points can be readily discerned. And this task is further complicated by the need to set out the two lines of reasoning in such a way that they also make contact with each other.

C. and **E.**   This last remark also implies a central constraint on the project of evaluating the two positions. What an adjudicatory essay requires is that the adequacy of each of the two positions be assessed from the standpoint of the other position. In the simplest sort of case, one of the two texts will actually be a direct critical commentary on the views and arguments developed in the other text. In such a case, the student will know what one of the two parties has to say about the considerations offered by his opponent in support of his competing views. But there still remains the job of figuring out what that opponent would say in defense of his views and, in particular, in reply to the criticisms offered by the first disputant. (Unfortunately, two philosophical texts cannot both be responses to each other.) This requires you, in the role of a potential adjudicator, to imaginatively place yourself in the shoes of that other philosopher—that is, to imaginatively think yourself into the systematic viewpoint on which the text draws and attempt to use the resources of that viewpoint as the base from which to mount your critical assessment. Doing this demands a certain sympathy on your part. It requires that you read each text for its strengths as well as for its weaknesses, and that you allow each of the disputing parties his or her strongest possible case. Only in this way will your proposed resolution capture what is worth preserving from the two positions, as well as making it clear what should be abandoned from each. Only in this way, in short, can your philosophical adjudication result in the clarification of authentic and substantial questions, rather than consisting in argumentatively knocking over straw figures that you have constructed from the texts in the first place only to serve as easy critical targets.

F.   Only rarely will the final resolution of a philosophical disagreement amount to a judgment that one or the other of the disputing parties is wholly correct. More typically, what is called for is a careful interweaving of complementary insights suggested by the two texts, perhaps supplemented by some of the student's own. A thorough critical exploration of competing positions often reveals that the initially formulated question actually rests upon a complex structure of presuppositions. What begins as a single question may unpack into a large family of issues, some approached more fruitfully by one of the disputants and some by the others. Frequently what one most needs to do is to construct and apply an assortment of distinctions—for example, among different ways of reading some text, or among different senses that can be assigned to some term, or among different interpretations that can be placed upon some fact, argument, or remark. And even in those cases where no particular positive answer to a given question is clearly defensible, it is often possible to call attention to conceptual pitfalls and to mark sterile or misleading lines of reasoning that have been or might naturally be pursued on that question—and this is often no less useful than obtaining some defensible positive result.

A well-turned adjudicatory essay, then, makes substantially greater demands on a student than does the critical examination of a single view. Like such a critical examination, an adjudicatory essay requires mastery of dialectical technique. But, in addition, it also asks a student to attempt constructively to conduct at least one side of the discussion from a philosophical standpoint within which he or she does not naturally feel at home, and that requires a higher standard of sympathetic exegesis and philosophical imagination than what is typically needed for a purely critical task. An adjudicatory essay, then, takes one step along the road toward lessening what often strikes students as the extreme negativity of the practice of philosophy, for it calls upon them to understand each of a pair of competing philosophical positions well enough to appreciate its strengths as well as its shortcomings. It calls upon them, if only for a moment, to become advocates of some view other than their own. Once students begin in this way to grasp the range of possible philosophical advocacies, they have taken an essential step forward toward coherently developing their own philosophical world views and becoming articulate and effective proponents of them.

Philosophical Essays: Solving a Problem

Our third species of philosophical essay, like the second, is issue-oriented. The solution of a problem, however, draws more heavily on a student's originality and creative insight than on his or her exegetical and interpretive skills. Philosophical problems range from classical perplexities that have been unfolding through thousands of years of dialectical ramifications to brief set pieces constructed as exercises and illustrations. An essay devoted to one of the classical themes may nowadays be a fairly long book, whereas a classroom puzzle can usually be dealt with satisfactorily in a couple of pages. In either case, however, there will be a discernible structure to the writing which, predictably, I shall now proceed to discuss.

Like an adjudicatory essay, a problem-solving essay can usefully be regarded as having six parts:

A. Formulation and analysis of the problem
B. Development of criteria of adequacy for a solution
[C. Exploration of possible but inadequate solutions]
D. Exposition of the proposed solution
E. Assessment of the adequacy of the proposed solution.
[F. Replies to anticipated criticisms]

Again, you shouldn't regard this structural breakdown as permanently chiseled in granite. The brackets around items C. and F., for instance, are intended to indicate that these are genuinely optional components of a problem-solving essay, and what I have here separated out as A. and B. will often be tangled together in a single passage or series of passages, and still other modifications are possible. But the six-part structure I've outlined above is at least *one* useful way to think through and organize a problem-solving essay; and, as a beginning student of philosophy, you would be well advised to keep it in mind, at least until you have developed some facility with the form.

I want to expand on this bare structural outline—not, as I did in the last chapter, by providing an abstract discussion of each point, but by trying to exhibit the scheme in action. Here then is an example of the sort of compact and manageable problem that might be posed as a homework assignment for an introductory philosophy class.

(Long ago, I actually used it in that way, and I did hate to part with it, but it's still doing service in a good pedagogical cause.):

> Astronomers tell us that it takes four years for light to reach us from the nearest star. But during those four years, the star may have ceased to exist, and we can't see what doesn't exist. Do we ever see a star?

I propose to work through this little problem step by step according to the six-part scheme that I've sketched. What I plan to do is try to take it nice and slow, so that you can follow, I hope, the process of *thinking* that leads up to such results as there are.

Before I begin, however, let me pause briefly to address a question which perhaps occurred to you as you read the problem: Why bother? Who cares whether or not we ever see a star? Early in this book, you may recall, I made a variety of remarks about a sense of liberation and joy that can be achieved through the practice of philosophy—but what does *this* problem have to do with liberation and joy?

By itself, alas, not much. This handbook, after all, is concerned primarily with technique, and the sort of problem that recommends itself on pedagogical grounds as a good vehicle for illustrating certain points of technique is likely to be a rather unexciting one. The exciting ones are the complicated ones, you see, and the technical points tend to get lost among the complications. So there are, in fact, good pedagogical reasons for selecting a "Who cares?" type of problem as an illustrative example.

But there's something else that it's important to say at this point. *Excitingness* isn't a property of a thing as is its color or size or shape. Whether or not something is exciting depends on what you can do with it, on how it connects up with other things that you care about. A footprint or a fingerprint or a cigarette butt isn't usually terribly interesting in its own right—but when it's a key clue that reveals the identity of a murderer, the discovery of a footprint or some such trivial thing can be very exciting indeed. Now if you're new to the philosophy game, you probably don't have very much on your intellectual agenda that you can connect up with this little problem. It just sits there, a pointless exercise in a textbook. Well, I understand, and I can sympathize with you, but there isn't very much I can do about that here.

Suppose, however, that you'd embarked upon the project of trying to achieve a comprehensive and coherent overview of the nature and limits of human knowledge—surely at least potentially an exciting prospect. One of the main regions you would need to map would be the territory marked "perception," a territory encompassing seeing and hearing, feeling and smelling and tasting. Many roads crisscross and wander through this terrain. Some are the rough, old, worn dirt footpaths that I earlier called "common sense." Others, however, are new, clean, tidy paved tracks laid down by the special sciences—neuroanatomy, physiological psychology, biophysics, and the like. Sometimes these roads cross harmoniously—there is an overpass or an underpass—or run along parallel to one another. But sometimes they clash—there is an impasse. And when this happens, your effort to attain that joyful and liberating coherent understanding of human knowledge in general and, less generally, of perception and, in particular, of *seeing* is blocked. Before you can get a picture that hangs together, you have a problem to solve, a conceptual knot to untie.

The little puzzle about seeing stars *can* be part of such a problem. And if it is, if you encounter it *in that context*, then you will no longer be inclined to ask "Why bother?" For the puzzle will then not be merely an exercise. It will be an *obstacle*—and the larger project that moves you, the goal of a coherent understanding that draws you onward, will supply all the reasons for bothering that you could ever need or want.

This handbook cannot supply you with such a living context. No book can. Such things must arise from within you, from your own need or desire to understand something. The most I can do for you here is show you how to proceed, how such a (small) conceptual knot can be unraveled. The most I can teach you is technique; the rest you must supply for yourself. And that takes time, and it takes experience. Our intellectual projects are not dictated to us. One day, we simply *find* ourselves with them; and we and they grow and mature together.

So much, then, for apologetics. The proper thing to do now is to begin.

A.   What *is* the problem here anyway? There's obviously a specific question being asked: "Do we ever see a star?" Is *that* the problem? It hardly seems likely. *Of course* we see stars, one is surely tempted to answer. On a clear night we can see hundreds of them. What seems to be more problematic is the suggestion of an *argument* that looks like it's trying to demonstrate that at least some of the times when we think we're seeing a star, we're actually *not*. Let's see if we can tease out the details of that argument.

What's the relevance of the fact that light from stars takes years to reach us? Who cares about the light? Well, it hooks up with *seeing*, doesn't it? What's evidently being appealed to here is a bit of fairly simpleminded science. I don't see anything unless light from it enters my eyes and stimulates my retinas, triggering certain electrical events in my optic nerves and, ultimately, causing appropriate electrochemical changes in the visual cortex of my brain. So *if* we see a star, we don't see it until the light it emits arrives here, where we are, and acts on us.

The puzzle's next observation is that a star may have ceased to exist while its light was on the way to us. Well, let's suppose that this happened; the star exploded or something. It's then supposed to follow that we *don't* see the star, because, the problem statement continues, "we can't see what doesn't exist." Is that right?

Let's think about it. Often we distinguish between (really) seeing something and merely *seeming* to see it. One of the things that makes a difference here (although not the only thing) is whether or not the thing we *think* we're seeing actually exists. If it seemed to me that I saw an oasis on the horizon or a pink elephant pirouetting in the corner, and I later discover that there *wasn't* any oasis or elephant there, I can't properly go on saying that I *saw* an oasis or a pink elephant. What I need to say instead is something like, "Well, I sure *thought* I saw an oasis (a pink elephant). I guess it was a mirage. (I guess I was hallucinating.)" It appears to be true, in other words, that we can't coherently *both* claim to really see something *and* grant that what we seem to see doesn't actually exist. The most we can correctly say in such a case is, "It's just *as if* I were (really) seeing it." It seems fair to agree, then, that we can't see (really, genuinely *see*) what doesn't exist. If what we *think* we're seeing doesn't exist, then we're not actually seeing it. We only seem to be.

But can we extract a philosophical problem from all these remarks? I think we can. Let's start with the claim that we see stars all the time and know perfectly well that we do. We can assign that claim to the loose family of beliefs that I earlier called "common sense." It certainly seems to belong there. Now, drawing on what our bit of amateur science tells us about stars and seeing, we can construct two possible scenarios, both of which can fit one of those occasions on which we *think* we're seeing a star:

> *Case 1:* Light emitted from a star some years ago acts on us and causes us to have the experience that we call "seeing a star." Nothing untoward has happened to the star. It's just where it seems to be.
>
> *Case 2:* Light emitted from a star some years ago acts on us and causes us to have the experience that we call "seeing a star." However, sometime during the intervening years the star exploded, and now it no longer exists. There is now actually nothing at all where there seems to be a star.

In Case 1, we do see a star. But in Case 2, since we can't see what doesn't exist, we don't see a star. And now we can discern at least *a* problem: We can't tell the two cases apart. That is, we can't tell whether a particular experience of *seeming* to see a star is an example of Case 1 (*actually* seeing a star) or Case 2 (*merely* seeming to see a star). How could we? What happens to *us* (to our retinas, our optic nerves, and so on), and the experience we have because of it, is identical in both cases. So, for all we actually *know*, it might be true that all those occasions on which we seem to see a star are in fact of the Case 2 sort—and if so, we never would see a star. For all we actually *know*, we never actually *do*.

The underlying problem, then, is an apparent clash between common sense and contemporary science. Although it's been very crudely drawn, the conflict goes roughly like this: Common sense proposes that we know perfectly well that we sometimes see stars. Scientific inquiry, in contrast, has uncovered a bunch of facts about stars and about seeing that, together, seem to imply that we in fact *can't* know whether we ever see a star. One question that we might profitably address in a short problem-solving essay, then, is how this apparent conflict might be resolved.

B.   Well, if that's our problem, what's wanted by way of a solution? What would we like to be able to accomplish in our essay? The most agreeable outcome would surely be one which preserves our initial confidence in *both* our unsophisticated common sense *and* our amateur science. In any event, we're not qualified to quarrel with the science. If some physiologist claims that light must impinge on the retina before a person can see anything, for instance, we have no grounds on which to disagree with her. We lack the relevant professional expertise. So one condition of adequacy we might lay down for a solution is that it recognize that stars are trillions of miles away, that light takes years to travel from them to us, that we see a star *if at all* only when light emitted from it has acted on us, and so on. But let's see if we can't salvage that little piece of common sense, too. It would be nice if it turned out that we often *do* see stars and know perfectly well that we do. So let's try requiring that any adequate solution treat that claim, too, as true. We want a solution, then, that claims we've been calling "common sense" as well as those we've been calling "science." There's no guarantee that a solution to the puzzle that endorses all those claims in fact exists, of course, but it's worth a try.

C.   If we adopt these restrictions on a solution, then there's one very tempting proposal that we can dismiss right away. This is the proposal that we *don't* really see stars; what we *really* see is the *light* emitted by the stars. This proposal might save our science, all right, but it does so at the price of our common sense, and we've decided to try not to do that. In fact, however, there are lots of independently good reasons not to succumb to this tempting proposal. Having a look at them might give us a clue as to how we might solve our original problem.

For one thing, if we never see stars but only the light they emit, then we never see anything *but* light, emitted or reflected. There's nothing special about *stars* in that respect. We don't see *anything* unless light from it suitably stimulates our retinas. Now that might still seem like a conclusion that we could live with—but let's reflect for a moment on the reasons that researchers have for accepting what we've been calling the claims of science in the first place. How did someone *find out* that we don't see anything unless and until the light that it emits or reflects acts on us? Presumably, whoever discovered this did so, among other things, by *making observations*. But if we never see anything but *light*, then no one has ever seen the meters, dials, telescopes, microscopes, mirrors, lenses, and other apparatus that were surely needed to make those observations, nor, for that matter, has anyone ever seen an eye or a retina or an optic nerve. So the very (scientific) facts that were supposed to imply that we don't ever see anything but light turn out to be facts that we couldn't *know* if it were true that we didn't ever see anything but light.

In fact, we might argue, the view that all we ever actually see is light rests on a straightforward confusion between *what* we see and *how* we see it. Granted that we don't see anything until the light that it emits or reflects acts on us, that tells us only *how* we see something. We see it *by means of* the light that it emits or reflects. *What* we see, however, is the object that emits or reflects the light. The light is the *medium* of sight, not the object of sight.

Indeed, the same sorts of considerations that suggested that we see only light would also seem to imply that we see only our own eyes. For, after all, we don't see anything unless and until our eyes are suitably stimulated—and "like premises support like conclusions." But again, what we should say here is that that's *how* we see something, not *what* we see. The eyes are the *organs* of sight, not its objects. (And in fact, if you think about it for a moment, you should realize that one thing you *can't* ever see is your own eyes—in contrast to, for example, seeing their reflection in a mirror. Where would you stand?)

So the tempting proposal is one that we should pass by. But it gives us a clue to the relevant problem-solving philosophical methodology, for it suggests that what may be called for is the careful drawing of a distinction like the one between what we see and how we see it. Perhaps there's some *other* distinction that we've been overlooking.

D. In the first part of my discussion, you will recall, I used the original formulation of the problem to produce a little *argument*. (Whether you think I extracted that argument or constructed it will depend upon how imaginative you thought I was being.) What we need to do is get inside that argument. In particular, we need to take a more careful look at the crucial extra premise: "We can't see what doesn't exist." Earlier, I briefly defended this principle by pointing out the commonsensical distinction between really seeing something and merely seeming to see something. In that defense, I appealed to the examples of mirages and hallucinations. But now, thinking in terms of drawing distinctions, it may occur to you to look for some way in which such cases are importantly *different* from that of an exploded star. ("No distinction without a difference.") And once you've put the question in this way, it almost answers itself. In the case of the mirage, there *never is* an oasis at that spot in the desert where there *appears* to be one, and in the case of the hallucination, there never is a pirouetting pink elephant in the corner where there appears to be one. But in the case of an exploded star, there *once was* a star in that region of space where there appears to be one. It's just that there isn't one there *now*. So we might distinguish what never exists (what doesn't exist at all, at any time) from what doesn't exist at the time we're having our visual experience.

This gives us two readings for our key premise, "We can't see what doesn't exist." We could read it as

(i)   We can't see what doesn't exist at the time we seem to see it.

Or we could read it as

(ii)   We can't see what *never* exists.

But which reading is at work in our argument? The answer seems to be: Both! For what I needed in Case 2 in order to conclude that we don't see a star was reading (i), but it is reading (ii) that I defended by citing mirages and hallucinations and by contrasting actually seeing with merely seeming to see. What that defense showed us was that there's some reason to accept the crucial premise as true *on reading (ii)*, but we've seen *no reason at all* to accept it if we interpret it according to reading (i). And that gives us a way to solve our original problem.

E. What we wanted to do was to preserve our common-sense conviction that we often do see stars and know perfectly well that we do without challenging any of the further claims about stars and seeing that arise from investigations in the natural sciences. Provided that we have a sufficiently refined understanding of our extra premise, we are now in a position to do this. Return again to our apparent clash between science and common sense. The problem that we decided to address, you will recall, was generated from three conclusions:

(c1)   In Case 1, we do see a star.

(c2)   In Case 2, we don't see a star.

(c3)   We can't tell the two cases apart.

But we can now see that there is a way open to us to reject the argument that led to (c2). We argued for (c2) on the ground that we can't see what doesn't exist. Since, however, in Case 2 there *once was* a star where there appears to be one, that conclusion will follow only if we interpret this key premise according to reading (i), as "We can't see what doesn't exist at the time we seem to see it"—and we are free to reject that interpretation. Our consideration of examples of things we merely seem to see, mirages and hallucinations, gave us only reasons to accept reading (ii), "We can't see what *never* exists"; but on that interpretation of the key premise, we no longer have any reason to accept (c2). When the premise is read *that* way, it no longer supports that conclusion. We can, therefore, consistently hold that we see a star *both* in Case 1 *and* in Case 2, and no conflict remains to disturb us.

F.   It might be objected that this solution doesn't provide us with any way of telling whether any particular experience of seeming to see a star is a Case 1 or a Case 2 type of experience. And this is correct. But it is not an *objection*. Our inability to distinguish between the two kinds of case was a *problem* only because we thought that the difference between the two cases was the difference between seeing a star and *not* seeing a star. Since we now understand that we can consistently reject that conclusion, we may contentedly reply to this "objection" by remarking that reaching a verdict about a particular experience always requires particular investigation. Of course it does. In this instance, the relevant investigative procedure is straightforward enough: Just wait the appropriate number of years. If the star has meanwhile exploded, sooner or later we'll get a look at the explosion—when the light from *it* reaches us. But there's no reason to suppose that we can tell whether we're in Case 1 or in Case 2 *just* by examining the single experience we're having at the time. That's neither "common sense" nor science. In fact, the same thing is true of experiences of seeing, as opposed to mirages and hallucinations and the like. We can't tell just by examining the *single* experience we're having that there isn't an oasis at that spot on the horizon or a pink elephant pirouetting in the corner. We need to go and check it out.

But it might be objected that it's still possible that *all* the cases in which we think we're seeing a star are Case 2 types of experiences—or, even worse, that in *all* the cases in which we think we're seeing *anything*, what's really going on is that we're hallucinating. Well, this gets us into deeper dialectical waters, but I can make two brief remarks that serve at least to defuse the immediate objection. On the one hand, it might indeed be the case that all the stars we will be seeing tonight exploded simultaneously, say about two years ago. No amount of pure armchair reasoning can guarantee that it didn't happen. In that event, we'd be in Case 2 with a vengeance. In fact, I would suppose that astronomers and astrophysicists have some excellent reasons for believing that it's extremely unlikely that any such thing happened, but that's quite beside the *philosophical* point. Even if there has been such a cosmic explosion, since we now understand that we can consistently hold that Case 2 experiences are instances of seeing stars, we still don't need to give up any of the common-sense or scientific claims at issue in our little puzzle. (Of course, the *non-philosophical* consequences of such a stellar explosion would remain a matter of legitimate and grave concern—but one quite beyond the scope of this book.)

And as for the more troublesome possibility of "universal hallucination" . . . well, how is the reasoning supposed to go? It looks to me as if it consists of two steps:

(Step 1) We can't tell by examining a single experience we're having whether or not it's an hallucination.
 · So, any experience could be an hallucination.

(Step 2) Any experience could be an hallucination.
 So, it could be the case that all experiences are hallucinations.

And if this *is* how the reasoning goes, then we're not in trouble. Step 1 may or may not be okay, but if you think about Step 2 for a minute, you'll discover that you already know what to say about it.

This concludes my commentary on our little puzzle and, with it, my general discussion of the problem-solving essay. It's interesting to note how easily such a minor philosophical set piece of this sort can open out into much larger questions regarding the reliability of sensory perception in general and the relative authoritativeness of common sense and empirical science, viewed as potentially competing codifications of what we properly know. This is a further reflection of the systematic and dialectical character of philosophical viewpoints on which I've earlier remarked. Any philosophical picture is, at least implicitly, a total world view, and a tug on any dangling thread vibrates the whole web.

There are a couple of specific observations that you should carry away from the discussions in this chapter. Probably the most important of these is how much of the work consists in clarifying just what the problem *is*. That's by far the largest of the six parts in my example, and this isn't at all extraordinary. It's quite typical. Only when we reconstructed the set problem as a conflict of arguments based in science and in common sense could we see where conceptual pressure needed to be brought to bear on it. And our detailed analysis of the problem was also what suggested criteria of adequacy sufficient to steer us away from the tempting, but ultimately confused, suggestion that we really see only light.

In short, time spent in spelling out a problem, in laying bare and making fully articulate the presuppositions and principles underlying the set question, is always time well spent. It is better to invest your energies in such a detailed formulation and analysis than to batter yourself to pieces on the rocks of a problem for lack of a genuine understanding of what the problem is. The point is sufficiently important and sufficiently complicated to deserve a more extensive discussion. For sometimes there's a twist. Sometimes what you finally need to talk about isn't the problem that *presents* itself, the question that seems, so to speak, to be floating on the expository surface. Sometimes you need to *dive* for your questions. And that really needs a chapter of its own.

CHAPTER ELEVEN

Diving for Questions: Beneath the Expository Surface

In the preceding chapter, I observed that the largest and most important part of your encounter with a philosophical problem frequently consists in getting clear about just what the problem *is*, and I suggested that doing so typically requires that you penetrate beneath the expository surface to expose, articulate, and examine the specific and general presuppositions on which the problem's superficial formulation tacitly rests. Often, when you've done so, the actual heart of the problem turns out to lie at some distance from where it originally *seemed* to be.

It is unfortunately not easy to describe the process I have called "getting clear about just what the problem is"—and, as usual, quite impossible to reduce it to a quasi-mechanical algorithm or recipe. The general strategy, however, is clear enough. It is to confront the various elements of the *statement* of the problem with what I earlier described as the characteristically philosophical concerns of making sense and establishing entitlements. A philosophical problem may *arise* from initially inchoate feelings and impulses, from Aristotle's sense of wonder, but its expression and articulation ultimately take the form of a *text*, a series of descriptions and hypotheses, claims and inquiries. To get *clear* about the problem, then, what you need to do is *interrogate* that text. You try to ensure that you understand its various descriptions and claims by asking of their key terms and the central concepts to which they appeal, "What does it mean?"—that is, "How might one explain the *sense* of these terms or the application of these concepts?" And you try to bring its various hypotheses and inquiries into sharp focus by pressing the question of *grounds*, "How could one tell?"—that is, "What would count as supporting evidence for such an hypothesis or as a satisfactory answer to such an inquiry?"

As usual, the only way to master these strategies for the clarification of problems is by putting them into practice, and as always, that is something you will need to do for yourself. What I can do for you here, however, is *illustrate* these strategies, and as usual, the best way to do that is with an example. Here, then, is a story for you:

> I've been a heavy cigarette smoker for quite a long time. On a number of occasions I've tried to quit, but it's never worked out. I've always started up

again after a fairly short time. A few days ago, however, I was again reflecting on the risks to my health from smoking and on what it was doing to my lungs, and I started getting rather seriously concerned about it. So I said to my good friend Eddie, "You know, I really want to quit smoking. This time I'm going to give it up for good." And Eddie said to me,

> *You?* Give up smoking? That's a laugh! I've known you for over twenty years, and you've smoked at least two packs a day during all that time. Of course you *want* to quit smoking, but you *can't;* you're hopelessly addicted. You like to *think* that you could still quit any time you wanted to, but you're just deluding yourself. You've known very well for years that you're slowly committing suicide every time you light up a cigarette. You've *tried* to quit a dozen times—and failed every time. None of that has made the slightest difference. You couldn't quit now if your life depended on it (which, alas, it does).

Well, as you can imagine, I was pretty disturbed by this, but I got to thinking about it and the more I thought about it, the more it started to look as though, sad to say, Eddie was probably right about me. So the next day, when I lit up a cigarette and my good friend Winnie said to me, "I really wish you'd quit smoking. I hate to see you poisoning yourself with those things," I explained to her about how I really *wanted* to give up smoking, but that, lamentably, I was addicted to cigarettes and consequently *couldn't* quit. And Winnie replied,

> That's the silliest thing I've ever heard you say. Of course you could quit, if you *really* wanted to. The problem is that you don't really want to. If you really wanted to quit, then you *would* quit. All this talk about "addiction" is just so much rationalization. You might like to *think* that you can't quit, but you're just deluding yourself. So-called "addicts" quit all the time. If you truly appreciated the damage that you're doing to your body, if you genuinely cared about the crud that's accumulating in your lungs, then you'd *really* want to quit . . . and then you would.

Well, I thought about that too, and darned if it didn't start to seem reasonable to believe that Winnie was probably also right about me. But surely they couldn't *both* be right. So who *is* right, Eddie or Winnie?

Eddie and Winnie obviously disagree about something. Indeed, at first encounter it seems that they disagree about almost everything. Their only apparent point of agreement is that I'm deluding myself—but even here there seems to be no agreement at all regarding what I'm deluding myself *about*. On the face of it, there are two main candidates: whether or not I *want to* quit smoking, and whether or not I *can*. And, at first blush, Eddie and Winnie certainly *seem* to disagree about both of these questions. Eddie at least explicitly *says* that I do want to quit, but also that I can't; and Winnie, in contrast, explicitly *says* that I can quit, but also that I don't really want to. Finally, the story concludes with a question of its own—Who is right?—

presumably addressed precisely to these competing claims. Both the central dis-agreements and the leading question at issue in this story, in short, certainly *seem* straightforward enough. Have we then gotten sufficiently clear about what the prob-lem here actually *is*? Perhaps—but we can't be sure about that until we've conduct-ed our interrogation. Let's go diving.

Eddie, for instance, says that I'm *addicted* to cigarettes (or perhaps to nicotine). But just what does that mean? However familiar it might be, the notion of addiction is certainly not self-explanatory. Some people, for instance, are inclined to distinguish "physical addiction" from "psychological addiction"; others find such a distinction insupportable. Correlatively, some people limit the application of the concept to *sub-stances* (e.g., nicotine, heroin, alcohol); others are prepared to extend it to *activities* (e.g., gambling) as well. Again, the notion of addiction is often connected with, or even equated with, the notion of *dependency*. A person who is addicted to some sub-stance is said to be dependent upon that substance. But dependent upon it *for what*? Each of us is dependent upon air, water, and food, for instance, to remain alive, but Eddie obviously isn't claiming that my quitting smoking would prove fatal.

At least this much is clear from what Eddie says: Whatever "being addicted" ulti-mately amounts to, one thing it is evidently supposed to *imply* is that I *can't* quit smok-ing. I can't quit, Eddie says, even though I want to. I can't quit even if my life depends on it. In short, according to Eddie, I can't quit, period—whether I want to or not.

But what kind of 'can't' is this supposed to be? Eddie is surely not claiming that it's *logically impossible* for me to give up cigarettes. However unlikely or improba-ble it might be that it ever becomes true, the statement "J.F.R. has quit smoking" is clearly not self-contradictory. When Eddie says to me "You can't quit smoking," then, he's not saying something analogous to "You can't draw a four-sided triangle." That would be self-contradictory, but this logical 'can't' is not what's at issue here.

Nor is Eddie claiming that it's *physically impossible* for me to quit smoking. The notion of physical impossibility is correlative to the notion of *natural necessity,* the necessity of a *law of nature*. But not only is "J.F.R. quits smoking" not *self*-con-tradictory, it also doesn't contradict any such natural law. When Eddie says to me "You can't quit smoking," then, he's not saying something similar to "You can't fly just by flapping your arms." That would be contrary to the laws of physics and biol-ogy, but this physical 'can't' is plainly also not what's at issue here.

But then, just what *is* Eddie saying when he says that I *can't* quit smoking? It's beginning to look as if 'can't' may be out of place here. At first encounter, Eddie's appeal to the notion of addiction looked like part of a solid *explanation* of my con-tinuing to smoke: The fact that I was addicted implied that I *couldn't* quit smoking, and the fact I *couldn't* quit implied that I *didn't*. But our failure so far to locate a sense of 'can't' in which it's true to say that I can't quit suggests that the concept of addiction simply doesn't carry that sort of explanatory weight. My "being addicted" to nicotine perhaps implies that it is extremely *unlikely* that I will give up cigarettes, that it would be very *difficult* for me to quit smoking, that quitting would be extraor-dinarily *unpleasant* (e.g., accompanied by disagreeable or even painful "withdrawal symptoms")—but the truth of all that, of course, is entirely compatible with its *also* being true that I *can* quit smoking. And if, after all, I can quit, and if I really want to quit (as I sincerely believe I do), then Eddie's remarks do not yet explain why I don't quit. After all, *some* people who are "addicted" to cigarettes actually *do* quit. Nor, once we have sorted through Eddie's remarks in this way, does there seem to be very much left over that Winnie would still disagree with, although she might certainly put it differently.

Winnie, in any case, evidently doesn't think much of Eddie's appeal to the notion of my "being addicted" at all. She calls it a "rationalization." What Eddie calls 'addiction', she's apparently more inclined to treat as simply a *very bad habit*, one that's both harmful or self-destructive and also extremely difficult to break. But "extremely difficult" does not imply *impossible*. Of course I *could* quit smoking if I wanted to. If I don't quit, then, the reason can only be that, despite my sincere assertions to the contrary, I *don't* want to quit—or, as Winnie prefers to put it, I don't *really* want to. As she sees it, my problem is not "addiction." My problem is rather something more like "weakness of will." My desire to quit smoking just isn't *strong* enough; my resolve to give up cigarettes doesn't have enough "oomph" behind it.

But is Winnie's claim that I "don't really want to" quit actually any clearer than Eddie's claim that I can't? What would count for Winnie as showing that I *did* "really want to quit"? For it needn't be the case that I've been, so to speak, halfhearted about the matter. I have, after all, repeatedly *tried* to quit smoking. Thereby, let us suppose, I have subjected myself to any number of difficult and disagreeable experiences. I wore nicotine patches; I checked myself into clinics; I joined twelve-step programs—but all to no avail. Sometimes, to be sure, I did manage to go for a short time without cigarettes, but after a week or a month or two, there I was, smoking again. And if, after all this, Winnie continues to insist that I could quit for good "if I really wanted to," can we still understand her? Commonsensically, it can be true that (1) I really want to do something; (2) I sincerely try to do it; and (3) I nevertheless fail. But can Winnie distinguish in this commonsensical way between the question of whether or not I "really want to" do something and the question of whether or not I *actually succeed* in doing it?

Or, again, what does it mean to say that my desire to quit smoking isn't "strong enough"? Strong enough for what? It seems that the answer has to be something like: Strong enough to guarantee that I actually *do* give up cigarettes. The question of whether or not my desire to do something is "strong enough," then, apparently turns out to be indistinguishable from the question of whether or not I "really want to" do that thing. Just as it seems that, as long as I'm still smoking, no amount of effort on my part is sufficient to convince Winnie that I "really want to quit," so, too, apparently nothing short of my successfully quitting can convince Winnie that my desire to quit smoking is "strong enough."

Commonsensically, the notion of "not being strong enough" is first of all at home in contexts where what is at issue is *physical* strength. Suppose, for instance, that a particular weight lifter (call him Samson) has frequently lifted 180 kilograms, occasionally lifted 190 kilograms, and once or twice even managed to lift 195 kilograms—but that despite intensive training and repeated attempts, he has not once succeeded in lifting 200 kilograms. Samson, we might naturally enough say, isn't strong enough to lift 200 kilograms. Like Eddie's appeal to the notion of addiction, this remark initially look likes it's offering an *explanation* of Samson's failure to do something. But how is the explanation supposed to go? Strength, after all, isn't a kind of *stuff*, like fuel. Samson's not being strong enough to lift 200 kilograms isn't like an automobile's not having enough fuel in its tank to travel 200 miles. The amount of fuel in an automobile's tank can be measured *independently* of the distance it's able to travel; but there is no analogous independent measure of Samson's strength, that is, independent of the weight-lifting performances and similar achievements—"feats of strength," as they are called—that from time to time he actually carries out.

To say that Samson isn't strong enough to lift 200 kilograms, then, isn't to offer an explanation of some phenomenon. Such a remark functions more like a description coupled to a prediction. It *summarizes*, as it were, Samson's weight-lifting track record to date—the fact that he has repeatedly tried to lift 200 kilograms, but always failed—and it suggests that, if he were to try *again* to do so, he would *again* fail. At best, it may rule out certain *other* sorts of explanations.

Samson's case, for example, can be contrasted with that of another weight lifter, say "Hercules," who not long ago regularly managed to lift 200 kilograms (and from time to time even more)—and so is presumably "strong enough" to do so—but who *today* repeatedly "tops out" at 195. Hercules' failure to do today what he has successfully done recently might be explained in a variety of ways. Perhaps he's pulled a muscle or strained a ligament; perhaps he was out on the town last night and has a nasty hangover; perhaps he's just overtired. In any event, in light of his overall record of successes, it is appropriate to seek and to expect to find some such *specific* explanation of Hercules' most recent failures. In contrast, if we accept the claim that Samson "isn't strong enough" to lift 200 kilograms, we are evidently absolved of the responsibility to seek such a singular explanation of any of his failures. That claim, on the contrary, suggests that there is no such *specific* explanation to be found.

Winnie's claim that my desire to quit smoking "isn't strong enough" resembles the claim that Samson isn't strong enough to lift 200 kilograms. It too initially looks like an explanation—in particular, an explanation of why I *haven't* quit smoking. But just as there's no measure of Samson's *physical* strength independent of his actual weight-lifting performances, so too there's no measure of the strength of my desire to quit smoking (or of my "strength of will" for that matter) that's independent of the actual history of my attempts to quit and their *de facto* success or failure. Winnie's claim, too, is thus perhaps best understood as a kind of description-plus-prediction, a summary of my sad track record in the business of quitting smoking plus the suggestion that, if I *were* to try again to quit, I would *again* fail. And, come to think of it, isn't that just what Eddie would say?

For at this point we might naturally notice that, in addition to saying that Samson isn't strong enough to lift 200 kilograms, we could in such circumstances, speaking commonsensically, also say that it's turned out that Samson *can't* lift 200 kilograms. Our reflections on such a case may remind us, in other words, that in addition to expressing the notion of *possibility*, 'can' is also used to express the notion of a person's *ability*. Often, that is, what a person *can* do is what he or she is *able to* do. Correlatively, to say that Samson *can't* lift 200 kilograms is surely to say, not that it's logically or physically impossible for him to do so, but rather that, for whatever reason, he's *unable* to do so.

Sometimes, of course, the reason that a given person is unable to perform this or that task does have to do with logical or physical impossibility, in that the task's description may be self-contradictory or inconsistent with well-established natural laws. But sometimes it's both logically and physically possible for a person to do something and, for all that, he's nevertheless unable to do it. Here we can distinguish two possible cases, corresponding to two kinds of considerations that might be cited as evidence in support of the ascription of such an inability. I myself, for instance, am not able to speak Rumanian or walk a tightrope, not because it's logically or physically impossible but simply because I've never *learned how* to speak Rumanian or walk a tightrope. In this case, I *lack* the relevant abilities. That's the first possibility. But sometimes a person is unable to do something not because he lacks the ability to do it, but rather because his specific circumstances prevent him from *exercising* an ability which it still remains correct to say that he *has*. I *have* the ability to ride a bicycle, for instance—I rode one to the bakery this morning—but I can't do so in my present circumstances, that is, while seated in front of a computer in my office. No bicycle is available to me here. What I'm missing here is not the appropriate mastery of the skills required to perform the action in question—I'm a fully competent bicyclist—but rather something that is a (further, "external") *necessary condition* for my performing it. And that's the second possibility.

These observations give us another way to interpret Eddie's claim that I can't quit smoking. What he may be saying is not that it is logically or physically impossible for me to quit but rather that, for one or another reason, I'm *unable* to quit. But *why* am I unable to quit? That is, which sort of case does Eddie have in mind? Well, recall that he agrees that I really do *want* to quit smoking. Although it's plainly not sufficient, my wanting to quit is presumably *one* of the necessary conditions for my quitting. Indeed, in the particular circumstances, my wanting to quit is the most central and salient of the "internal" ("subjective," "psychological") conditions which would have to obtain before I actually quit. But it is also reasonable to suppose that Eddie doesn't believe I'm unable to quit because some *"external"* ("objective," "matter-of-factual") necessary condition of my doing so is missing. It's not obvious that there *are* any such "external" necessary conditions for quitting smoking. Let us posit, then, that from Eddie's point of view, *all* the necessary conditions for my quitting are satisfied. If I am unable to quit, then, it is because I lack the very ability to do so itself. And that gives us an alternative perspective on Eddie's appeal to the notion of addiction. His picture seems to be, roughly, that becoming addicted results in the loss of certain abilities. My addiction to nicotine has, so to speak, robbed me of the ability to quit smoking.

Looking at Winnie's remarks from this perspective, we can interpret her antipathy to the notion of addiction as arising from her conviction that, whatever else may be the case, nothing has deprived me of the *ability* to give up smoking. One's ability to modify one's own behavior, to stop doing something one has become accustomed to doing, is not something that can be canceled or switched off. Having such an ability is part of what it means to be an *agent* in the first place. If I have so far been *unable* to quit, then, it's not because I lack the ability to do so but only because some (further) condition necessary for the *exercise* of that ability has so far been missing. And surely what's at issue for Winnie is not a public "external" condition like a handy bicycle, but precisely the central and most salient personal "internal" necessary condition, the condition she calls "really wanting to" or "having a strong enough desire" to quit. I have the *ability* to quit, all right. What I lack is one of the things I need in order to *exercise* that ability. What I lack is the necessary *resolve*.

On this interpretation, then, Eddie and Winnie *agree* that I am *unable* to quit smoking. In light of my repeated failed attempts to do so, that conclusion seems eminently reasonable. What they apparently disagree about is the *reason* I am unable to quit. Eddie evidently thinks that I lack the ability to quit; Winnie insists that the problem is not a lack of ability but my failure to supply one of the "internal" factors necessary for its *exercise*—a "strong enough" desire to quit, the requisite determination.

But have we really made any progress here? The distinction between lacking an ability and lacking one of the conditions necessary for the exercise of that ability is clear enough in the case of such *learned* or *acquired* abilities as speaking Rumanian, walking a tightrope, or riding a bicycle, and such "*external*", objective, matter-of-factual necessary conditions as the availability of suitable conversational partners, appropriate footwear, or a functioning vehicle. As in the case of Hercules' weight lifting or my own bicycle riding, a past history of successful performances can render it plausible that an agent in fact possesses some specific ability; and an agent's new or renewed success, once a supposedly missing condition has been (re-)supplied, supports the hypothesis that what was previously lacking was not the ability *per se* but only something necessary for its exercise.

In the present case, however, the ability ostensibly at issue is an agent's ability to modify his or her own behavior—specifically, to stop doing something he or she once chose to begin doing; and the necessary condition that's supposed to be in question is "internal," subjective, or psychological—namely, that very agent's own desire, resolve, or determination. But on what grounds are we to choose between concluding (with Eddie) that I lack the ability to quit smoking and concluding (with Winnie) that, although I possess the ability, I lack the necessary determination or resolve to exercise it?

I do, of course, have a past history of success in stopping doing *some* of the things that I once chose to begin doing. I now wear a full beard, for instance, and so I no longer shave, although I did so for many years. I don't drink non-decaffeinated coffee after dinner any more, although I used to do so all the time. There are, indeed, *many* such examples of my voluntarily changing habits earlier acquired, and Winnie can draw on the evidence of such past successes to support her claim that my failure to quit smoking is thus not to be explained by a lack of ability. Whenever my resolve to change has been strong enough, she will point out, change has been no problem at all. But Eddie's claim is not that I lack the ability to stop doing *anything* I once chose to begin doing, but only that I lack the ability to stop doing *one particular thing* I once chose to begin doing—and it's also true that, despite many evidently sincere attempts to quit smoking, I have had absolutely *no* success in doing so. What better evidence could one have for a missing ability, Eddie might ask, than such an unbroken record of failures? Yet surely it's just here that Winnie will point to my *general* capacity as an agent to modify aspects of my own behavior, arguing that the record of failures shows only that I have not yet managed to muster the level of resolute determination necessary to exercise my innate ability for self-control in this particular, admittedly extremely difficult, matter. Some habits are just *harder* to break than others.

The more one thinks about this sort of case, in fact, the less there seems to be to choose between describing things Eddie's way—I'm addicted to nicotine and so lack the ability to quit smoking—and describing things Winnie's way—I have a bad habit that's especially hard to break and haven't yet succeeded in mustering sufficient resolution to do so. The available evidence appears to be the same in either case: my *general* history of competent and successful self-management as a rational agent and my dramatically contrasting *particular* history of attempts and failures in the matter of quitting smoking. Both Eddie and Winnie concede all this evidence, but each *interprets* it differently, and it's just not clear that one of those interpretations is any more or less plausible than the other. And now it might occur to us to ask: Well, what *difference* does it make if we interpret the evidence one way or another? What *turns on* the question of whether we describe things Eddie's way or Winnie's way?

Let's try thinking about the matter this way: Whose *fault* is it that I haven't stopped smoking, despite the fact that I know it's a nasty, unhealthy, and self-destructive habit? Eddie's answer, at least, is clear enough: It's *nobody's* fault. That is, it's no *person's* fault. It's the fault of the *stuff*, the nicotine or the tobacco. In particular, it's not *my* fault, for I have an *excuse* for my failures. I'm addicted to the stuff. And once we've become sensitized to this implication of Eddie's way of describing my situation, we can see that the point of disagreement between him and Winnie may have very little to do with *explanations* after all.

Out of an appropriate concern for my own health and longevity, stopping smoking is something that I *should* do. (Eddie and Winnie and I all agree about that.) To the extent that I fail to do what I should do, I'm open to criticism—unless I have a *legitimate excuse*. What Winnie plainly finds especially objectionable is my attempt (inspired by Eddie's remarks) to invoke the notion of addiction as such an excuse. That the substance in question causes physiological changes in consequence of which giving it up would be very *unpleasant* may indeed explain why it's *difficult* to give it up, but that doesn't get me off the hook. From Winnie's perspective, that is, I can legitimately be *held responsible* for my repeated failure to quit smoking. If something that I should do is especially difficult to do, then I'm just going to have to try harder.

Of course, Eddie can concede that it was unwise of me to *begin* smoking. I shouldn't ever have started, and so there's perhaps at least one thing for which I can be legitimately criticized. (On the other hand, Eddie may be inclined to cite excusing circumstances for that behavior as well: It's not my fault that I started smoking; I was simply another casualty of "stress" or "peer pressure" or "manipulative advertising" or just "society.") Be that as it may, Eddie's attitude toward my *present* smoking is clearly exculpatory. There's nothing wrong with my desires—I *want* to give up cigarettes—and there's nothing wrong with my beliefs—I'm perfectly aware that smoking is killing me. But in this instance, my normally effective beliefs and desires turn out to be completely impotent. In the matter of quitting smoking, I have become a *helpless victim*.

Winnie, in contrast, is evidently unwilling to absolve me of responsibility in this matter. In her view, the fault lies entirely *within me*. My beliefs are indeed defective—I don't really appreciate the damage I'm doing to myself—and, in consequence, I regularly fail to marshal a suitably strong and focused desire to quit. To put it another way, Winnie appears to be convinced that, despite my claims to the contrary, I am still, as it were, implicitly "of two minds" about the matter of smoking. What I need to do is, so to speak, *pull myself together*—to attend to what I do know about the effects and perils of smoking with sufficient *vividness* to bring my beliefs and my desires into appropriate accord with one another. And whether or not I do *that* is completely up to me. When I don't quit, then, the fault is entirely my own.

In this way, an ostensible *description* of a person's conduct can come to be seen as the expression of an implicit *appraisal* of that conduct. Correlatively, what initially appears to be a disagreement about matters of fact, a dispute regarding the correct explanation of a phenomenon, comes to be reinterpreted as a disagreement centered instead primarily in *practical attitudes*, such as the difficult and important business of assigning responsibility and allocating praise or blame. From this new perspective, the original question—"Who's right, Eddie or Winnie?"—is not asking for a theoretical explanation of my track record vis-à-vis quitting smoking, but rather which of two *practices* can be better *justified:* Winnie's holding me personally responsible for the damage I'm doing to myself by continuing to smoke or Eddie's letting me off the hook with a special excuse called "addiction." And when the question is understood in this way as a question of justifying this or that practice, its philosophical exploration ultimately leads us to issues quite different from considerations of possibility and ability. It becomes relevant, for instance, to inquire into the *point* of having such social practices as the ascription of responsibility and the acknowledgment of excuses in the first place.

Not every formulation of a philosophical problem, of course, merits this sort of extended interrogation: it is admittedly unusual for one's initial explorations of a problem-setting text to lead off in so many strikingly different and perhaps surprising directions. Even in philosophy, a question is *sometimes* just what it seems to be. But you should not on that account be too quick to rest content with your first, relatively unreflective interpretation of a problem that you've been asked to unravel. You may not need to put on the full scuba gear, but in light of the dialectical and systematic character of philosophical views, a bit of diving below the expository surface will almost always serve you in good stead. In any event, a sensitive analysis and interpretation of the set question in the interest of getting properly clear about what the problem is, structured by appropriate attention to the characteristically philosophical themes of making sense and establishing entitlements, is a *sine qua non* for a successful problem-solving essay. Along with writing critical examinations of various views and attempting to adjudicate some carefully selected disputes, undertaking to solve such set problems will be a central and important part of your own philosophical practice from the beginning. And the skills you develop in completing such exercises will prove indispensable if and when you finally come to attempt the fourth, final, and most difficult sort of philosophical essay.

CHAPTER TWELVE

Philosophical Essays: Defense of an Original Thesis

It is unlikely that you will be called upon as a student to articulate and defend a wholly novel philosophical conception. This is for the best. Unlike the forms of essay we've examined so far—critically examining a view, adjudicating a dispute, solving a set problem—the defense of an original thesis resists even the modest levels of pedagogical codification that we've so far been able to achieve. Of course, any such defense must contain an exposition of the proposed thesis or view, along with the development and presentation of a set of reasoned considerations in support of it. Frequently, the proponent of an original thesis will also want to anticipate and meet in advance certain natural criticisms of the view, ward off certain predictable misunderstandings, or elaborate upon the philosophical consequences—perhaps even the potential practical consequences—of accepting it.

Not infrequently, however, an original world view will also include a profoundly new *methodological* conception, a new metaphilosophy, which itself constrains the form of philosophical exposition. Moreover, a radically creative philosophical thesis may place severe demands upon the literary talents of its advocates. For such reasons, the influential major writings of the great philosophers are often moving literary works of extraordinary grace and power. They range in expository form from the spirited dialogues of Plato's Athenians to the crystalline geometry of Spinoza's *Ethics,* from the rigid architectonic structure of Kant's *Critique of Pure Reason* to the powerful mythic aphorisms of Nietzsche's *Zarathustra* or the seemingly loose collection of suggestive, often superficially unrelated, numbered paragraphs assembled by Wittgenstein as his *Philosophical Investigations.*

In short, when we turn from critique, adjudication, and problem solving to the theme of creativity in philosophy, we pass, as we inevitably do in *any* discipline, beyond the point at which our subject is teachable. I cannot give you any guidance as to how to write such works. The most that I can do is suggest some useful strategies for reading them. It is to this final topic, then, that I now turn.

CHAPTER THIRTEEN

Six Ways to Read a Philosopher

Philosophical writings are not for reading through; they are for reading down into. That is why the *contents* of philosophy courses—unlike the contents of, say, mathematics or biology courses—are not stratified by difficulty or complexity. In mathematics, for example, you need to master multiplication and division before geometry and algebra, geometry and algebra before trigonometry and calculus. In biology, you dissect an earthworm before a frog, a frog before a mouse. But in philosophy, you learn to crawl, to walk, and to run over the same landscape. In philosophy, one begins where one ends—with Plato and Aristotle, with Descartes and Hume, indeed with the whole galaxy of great philosophers, with their writings and their concerns. What varies throughout your development as a student of philosophy is not then, in the first instance, the objects of your intellectual encounters but the form and depth of your intellectual engagement. The writings of a philosopher, in short, can be read in many ways. Here are six:

1. You Can Read a Philosopher for Conclusions

This is probably the most common and natural first-time approach for a beginning student or amateur philosopher. You read a person's work to find out *what* he or she believes. You assemble a list of views and opinions. If one's investigation ends here, what comes out is the *taxonomic* (labeling) style of studying philosophy. Every philosopher gets assigned to an appropriate "ism"—realism, idealism, empiricism, rationalism, existentialism, utilitarianism, classicism, intuitionism, logicism, nominalism, and so on. The possibilities for classification and subclassification are endless. There is, in fact, some point to getting a handle on such groupings. They give you a rough, but still useful, overall map of the philosophical terrain. For someone who is interested in a piece of philosophical writing primarily as a cultural or historical artifact, as an episode in the history of ideas, this first approach to philosophical reading may well suffice. But for a genuine student of philosophy *per se*, it's only the beginning.

2.   *You Can Read a Philosopher for Arguments*

The crucial next step is to attempt to press beyond the content of a philosopher's conclusions, the theses and views that the philosopher endorses, to an appreciation of the structure of reasoning underlying and supporting those conclusions. Here you read a person's works to discover not just what he or she thinks, but *why* he or she thinks it. One beneficial byproduct of this approach is that it delivers an insight into the *connections* among a philosopher's view, the ways in which the various conclusions hang together or fail to hang together, support or undermine one another. A careful reading of a philosopher in this way, for the purpose of exposing, articulating, and understanding the structure of the reasoning, is an essential foundation for any further approach to philosophical works. But it is a foundation that can be built upon in various ways.

3.   *You Can Read a Philosopher in the Dialectical Setting*

Every philosopher enters our great historical conversation at some specific place and time. Every philosopher has predecessors and teachers, colleagues and opponents. The dialectical discussion, the activity of meeting arguments with arguments, is typically already well under way. One thing you can do with the raw materials obtained from reading for conclusions and for arguments is to attempt to sort out the specific *dialectical* contribution that a philosopher proposes to make. How does this philosopher think that the central concerns and problems of the discussion have been conceived, and in what new ways does he or she propose that we now interpret and engage them? What new questions get asked? What false trails are marked and blocked?

A major work by a great philosopher is a stone dropped into a pool of concepts and concerns. To read a philosopher in the dialectical setting is to examine the ripples that such a splash creates, and to explore the ways in which they cancel and reinforce the many other sets of ripples stirring the surface of the pool. A philosophical problem is changed by the touch of a great mind. What the problem was before, and what it has become, are the concerns of this third style of philosophical reading. If reading for conclusions is reading for *what* a person thinks, and reading for arguments is reading for *why* he or she thinks it, then reading in a dialectical setting is reading for *how* that person thinks—and this is by far the most difficult of the three tasks.

But so far all these modes of philosophical reading call only upon a reader's exegetical and interpretive skills—the ability to think oneself into a philosophical view, to understand it, to reconstruct the reasoning supporting it, and to discern its wider implications in its dialectical setting. As with writing philosophy, however, here too there is room for more than exegesis and interpretation.

4.   *You Can Read a Philosopher Critically*

The conclusions are there. You know what a given philosopher thinks. The arguments are there. You know why he or she thinks it. Once you understand what the conclusions and the arguments *are*, then you can proceed to *assess* them. This is the critical reading of philosophy. To do it, you need to enter into an active dialogue with the text. To each of the philosopher's positive views or claims, you can set the critical questions: Is it true? Does it follow? The answers at which you arrive, however, test more than the cogency of the philosophical viewpoint at issue. Significantly, in this mode of philosophical reading, your own understanding of that viewpoint is also put to the test. For to read critically you ultimately need to appreciate more than what a philosopher says and why he or she says it. You need to achieve an understanding, too, of what the philosopher *would* say in response to your exploratory questions and critical challenges. Only when you have achieved this sort of imaginative and sympathetic grasp of a philosophical position can the critical attitude be expected to yield more than superficial quibbles. Only then can your critique bear significantly on what is *essential* to the view in question. So you need to understand not just what and why and how a philosopher thinks. To read critically, you must also discern what *turns on* the view at issue. And, of course, you will usually not be the first to try. So, . . .

5.   *You Can Read a Philosopher Adjudicatively*

Approaching philosophical reading in this fifth way multiplies immensely the demands placed on your analytic skill, extrapolative insight, and critical acumen. An adjudicative reading approaches a philosophical work in its dialectical setting as a critical reading approaches it in isolation. The aim here is not merely to appreciate the novel turns that a philosopher has given to an old problem, but to attempt to gauge the *import* of that contribution, to assess the adequacy of the philosopher's own interpretations and criticisms of his or her predecessors and contemporaries, and to evaluate the fruitfulness of the philosopher's new questions and methods and of the new directions they give to philosophical inquiry.

Accomplishing this task requires something rather like a carefully controlled schizophrenia. You must move sympathetically within a *number* of philosophical viewpoints—often developed through strikingly different expository idioms and embodying radically divergent conceptions of philosophical problems and methodology. You must attempt imaginatively to take the role of each of the original participants and to rethink the dialectic in its entirety from *all* these viewpoints—and from your own dispassionate and impartial point of view as well. For what you are seeking is more than an appreciation of the new insights to be gained. It is no less important that old insights not be permanently lost. The adjudicative reader thus cannot initially approach the dialectic as a partisan, for the concern is to isolate and preserve everything within it that is of lasting philosophical value. And this sets the stage for our final possibility.

6.   *You Can Read a Philosopher Creatively*

When you can approach a philosophical work in this sixth way, you will have crossed a major conceptual watershed. You will have made its author's problems your own. Engaging a piece of philosophical writing will no longer be a mere academic exercise. You will be on a quest. There will be something about people and their relations to the universe as knowers and doers that you need to understand, some conceptual tangle that resists your unraveling. When you turn to the great philosophical figures of the past, then, it will be with the intention of exploring a wider range of conceptual options than you are capable of evolving on your own, and with the goal and the hope that, through this exploration, you will eventually find the way to your own resolution of the puzzles that are haunting you. More than this, however, cannot easily be said. For creative philosophical reading resists pedagogical codification no less than creative philosophical authorship—and for the same reasons. Once again, in short, we have managed to reach the limits of what is teachable.

Retrospect

Philosophy is a practice. Its mastery is the mastery of a cognitive skill, not the assimilation of a body of facts. Even at best, then, a handbook of this sort can have only limited value. A practicing philosopher is a conceptual craftsman. Ultimately, as with any other craftsmanly pursuit, philosophy can be mastered only through the doing of it. The beginnings of such mastery evolve only gradually out of a long and often frustrating series of failed attempts. Behind every masterwork of cabinetry lies an ancestry of disappointments, of wobbly bookcases and skewed sideboards. So, too, it is with philosophy.

A few hours before his execution, Socrates offered some reflections on pain and pleasure:

> What a queer thing it is, my friends, this sensation which is popularly called pleasure. It is remarkable how closely it is connected with its conventional opposite, pain. They will never come to a man both at once, but if you pursue one of them and catch it, you are nearly always compelled to have the other as well; they are like two bodies attached to the same head. I am sure that if Aesop had thought of it he would have made up a fable about them, something like this: God wanted to stop their continual quarrelling and when he found that it was impossible, he fastened their heads together; so wherever one of them appears, the other is sure to follow after. That is exactly what seems to be happening to me. I had a pain in my leg from the fetter, and now I feel the pleasure coming that follows it.[1]

The pain of bondage, Socrates observed, is not merely a prelude to the pleasure of release. Paradoxically, it is its indispensable precondition as well.

Philosophy is that way too, of course. Its frustrations are both preludes to and preconditions of its joys. Sadly, beginning students inevitably must live more with the agony of philosophy than with its ecstasy. But philosophy is worth staying with. For, unlike being released from the bondage of physical fetters, breaking through the encrustations of frustrated thought to a clear and coherent philosophical overview of some complex conceptual terrain is a distinctively *human* pleasure, one available

---

[1] Plato, *Phaedo,* trans. F. J. Church (Indianapolis, Ind., and New York: Bobbs-Merrill, 1951), p. 4.

only to us animals whose life is a life of speech and reason. You cannot experience it without being changed. What you discover, curiously enough, is the true locus of *relevance*. For what in the end is most relevant to *us* is not the mundane daily business of living and earning a living, but precisely the free and unrestrained activity of reason—for reasoning animals is what *we* uniquely are. And to grasp that truth is to make a part of you the conviction by which Socrates lived and for which he died: that the unexamined life is not worth living.

Appendix

Puzzles

1. It is sometimes said that space is empty, which means, presumably, that there is nothing between two stars. But if there is *nothing* between two stars, then they are not separated by anything, and thus they may be right up against one another, perhaps forming some peculiar sort of double star. We know this not to be the case, of course, so it follows that space isn't empty after all.

2. It has been suggested that one reason why cattle are so timid is that their eyes are so constituted that they see human beings and other animals much larger than they really are. Does this seem likely to you?

3. Descartes writes that "stars or bodies at a great distance appear to us much smaller than they are." How near would we have to be to stars in order for them to appear the right size (that is, the size that they actually are)?

4. Could a person who was blind from birth know what the word 'red' means? By the way, what does the word 'red' mean?

5. When it's 12:30 P.M. in Newark, what time is it on Neptune?

6. When a straight swizzle stick is placed in a glass containing a whiskey and soda, we observe that it looks bent. If we investigate further, we may discover that it feels straight. What we usually go on to conclude is that it looks different from what it is, although it still feels the way it is. But that's silly. There's no reason for not concluding instead that the stick is (now) bent. It only feels straight, but the way it looks is the way it is. It's the way it feels that is now different from what it is. Is that right?

7. "John Doe may be a relative, a friend, an enemy, or a stranger to Richard Roe, but he cannot be any of these things to the Average Taxpayer. He knows how to talk sense in certain sorts of discussions about the Average Taxpayer, but he is baffled to say why he could not come across him in the street as he can come across Richard Roe."
    Both Richard Roe and the Average Taxpayer may be male, thirty-four years of age, married, homeowners, and earning $9,500 per year. But Richard Roe can live in Davenport, Iowa, have a wife named Amy, drive a Buick, and have maple trees

growing in his front yard—and the Average Taxpayer can't. Of course, the Average Taxpayer can have 2.6 children and own 1.3 automobiles—and Richard Roe can't. How do you explain all of this?

8. Dogs can hear sounds that are too high for people to hear. Could there be sound too high for *any* animal to hear?

9. The Greek Sophist Protagoras was so convinced of his effectiveness as a teacher of law that he once trained a pupil at no charge, on the condition that the student pay his fee from the proceeds of the first court case he won. After he was trained, however, the student refused to begin legal practice, so Protagoras sued to recover his fee. In court, Protagoras argued that, win or lose, the student must pay—by the terms of their agreement if the student won the case, and by the verdict of the court if the student lost it. The clever pupil, however, replied that the payment was forfeit in either case—by the terms of their agreement if he lost the case, and by the verdict of the court if he won it. Does Protagoras get his fee or not?

10. Suppose Achilles runs ten times as fast as the tortoise and gives the creature a hundred yards' start. In order to win the race, Achilles must first make up for his initial handicap by running a hundred years. But when he has done this and has reached the point where the tortoise started, the animal has had time to advance ten yards. While Achilles runs these ten yards, the tortoise moves one yard ahead; when Achilles has run this yard, the tortoise is a tenth of a yard ahead; and so on without end. Achilles never catches the tortoise, because the tortoise always holds a lead, however small.

11. "If my mental processes are determined wholly by the motions of atoms in my brain, I have no reason to suppose that my beliefs are true. Hence, I have no reason for supposing my brain to be composed of atoms."

12. If you see some part of an apple but not every part of the apple, then you see not an apple but only part of an apple. Since no one ever sees every part of an apple, no one ever sees an apple. The argument isn't restricted to apples. Peaches, pears, plums, cars, books, and people—no one ever sees them. Indeed, no one ever sees anything. What's gone wrong here?

13. Giving a poor man a penny does not alter the fact of his poverty: If he was poor before you gave him a penny, he's poor after you gave him the penny. A man with one penny to his name is certainly poor. Give a poor man a penny and he's still poor. So, a man with two pennies is poor. The same with three pennies. And four pennies. But if one keeps on long enough, the fellow has billions and billions of dollars. And a man with billions and billions of dollars certainly isn't poor. Sure, something's gone wrong with our reasoning here—but where and what?

14. "Since there is only one God to worship, a person who worships a God cannot but worship the true God." Then what is all the fuss about?

15. "If you don't believe that there is a God who created and designed the universe, then you must believe that everything that happens and that ever has happened is one vast *accident.*" Is that right?

16. What I see depends upon the state of my sense organs. Physical objects do not depend upon the state of my sense organs. Therefore, I do not see physical objects.

17. The way we assess any rule of interference that is questioned is to examine a sample of inferences drawn in accordance with the rule and observe whether or not the rule has been successful. If in almost all cases the inference proved to be correct, we may properly argue that the rule of inference has been justified. Now the following rule has been used in a wide variety of cases and has proved highly successful:

R: *From* "All hitherto observed *A*'s have been *B*'s,"
Infer "*A*'s observed henceforth will probably also be *B*'s."

Therefore, we may conclude that it will probably continue to be successful in the future, and we are justified in continuing to use it.

18. A benevolent being would eliminate evil and suffering if he could and if he knew about them. An omniscient being would know about any evil or suffering; and, of course, an omnipotent being could eliminate evil and suffering if he wanted to. But God is supposed to be omniscient, omnipotent, and benevolent. Why, then, is there evil and suffering in the world?

19. No matter how good a universe God in fact created, he could always have created a better one, for there is no such thing as the best possible universe, just as there is no such thing as the highest possible integer. It follows that we can make no moral criticism of God, since there is nothing that we can blame him for having failed to do. Is this right?

20. Just as a dissonant chord can contribute to the overall beauty of a symphony, and just as ugly brushwork can contribute to the total aesthetic effect of a painting, so it may be that evil and suffering are necessary components for the best of all possible worlds. If so, then we cannot morally censure God for permitting them. Is this right?

21. Could two objects differ *only* in length?

22. We're all taught in elementary school that we can't add apples and oranges. We're also taught that we *can* add apples and apples. "2 apples + 2 apples = 4 apples" is supposed to be true. Well, you probably know how to peel or eat or throw apples. But just how does one *add* apples?

23. Either God exists or he doesn't. Neither claim can be proved true. Thus, we must wager. If we wager that God exists, and we are right, we win everything; if we are wrong, we lose nothing. If we wager that God doesn't exist, and we are wrong, we lose everything; if we are right, we win nothing but we also lose nothing. This is

clearly the opportunity of a lifetime. Any reasonably prudent person should be eager to bet that God exists, and thus to lead the life of a believer.

24.   One Friday, a professor announced to her class that on one of their five meeting days during the next week, she would administer to them a *surprise quiz*. The class would not know on which of the five days it would take place until the morning when it was actually to be given. One of her students argued as follows: "You cannot give the quiz on Friday, for if it had not taken place on one of the four earlier days, we would know on Thursday night that it was to be given on Friday, and it would not be a surprise. Similarly, it cannot be given on Thursday. Friday is out, so if it had not been given on one of the first three days, we would know on Wednesday night that it was due on Thursday. Again, it would not be a surprise. Obviously, the same sort of argument applies to Wednesday, Tuesday, and Monday. It follows that you cannot give a surprise quiz at all." The professor was puzzled. She had decided to give the quiz on Wednesday, and she was quite sure that the students didn't know that. But she found the student's argument convincing, so she canceled the quiz. Should she have?

25.   Does the box below contain a true sentence or a false sentence?

> The sentence in the box on page 119 of *The Practice of Philosophy* is false.

26.   If there are no such things as Santa Claus and the Tooth Fairy, then what are you talking about when you explain to a child that there are no such things as Santa Claus and the Tooth Fairy?

27.   Sometimes we think about the moon. What makes thinking about the moon thinking about the moon, and not thinking about anything else?

28.   Suppose that, in fact, no great person has ever been born in the Aleutian Islands. Which of the following will then be true?

(a) If Abraham Lincoln had been born in the Aleutian Islands, he would not have been a great person.
(b) If Abraham Lincoln had been born in the Aleutian Islands, at least one great person would have been born there.

Why?

29.   Motion cannot begin. For in order for a body to traverse a given space (or length), it must first traverse half of that length. But it cannot traverse that half unless it first traverses half of that (the quarter); and it cannot traverse the quarter unless it first traverses half of that (the eighth); and so on. Whatever distance we select, there is some other distance that must be traversed before it, and another before that, and so on. So, motion can never begin.

30.   Did you know that red roses turn yellow in a totally dark room? Of course, they turn red again if they're exposed to the least bit of light.

Passages

A. *Plato,* Meno

SOCRATES:	There are some who desire evil?
MENO:	Yes.
SOCRATES:	Do you mean that they think the evils which they desire to be good; or do they know that they are evil and yet desire them?
MENO:	Both, I think.
SOCRATES:	And do you really imagine, Meno, that a man knows evils to be evils and desires them notwithstanding?
MENO:	Certainly I do.
SOCRATES:	And desire is of possession?
MENO:	Yes, of possession.
SOCRATES:	And does he think that the evils will do good to him who possesses them, or does he know that they will do him harm?
MENO:	There are some who think that the evils will do them good, and others who know that they will do them harm.
SOCRATES:	And, in your opinion, do those who think that they will do them good know that they are evils?
MENO:	Certainly not.
SOCRATES:	It is not obvious that those who are ignorant of their nature do not desire them; but they desire what they suppose to be goods although they are really evils; and if they are mistaken and suppose the evils to be goods, they really desire goods?
MENO:	Yes, in that case.
SOCRATES:	Well, and do those who, as you say, desire evils, and think that evils are hurtful to the possessor of them, know that they will be hurt by them?
MENO:	They must know it.
SOCRATES:	And must they not suppose that those who are hurt are miserable in proportion to the hurt which is inflicted upon them?
MENO:	How can it be otherwise?

SOCRATES: But are not the miserable ill-fated?
MENO: Yes, indeed.
SOCRATES: And does anyone desire to be miserable and ill-fated?
MENO: I should say not, Socrates.
SOCRATES: But if there is no one who desires to be miserable, there is no one, Meno, who desires evil; for what is misery but the desire and possession of evil?
MENO: That appears to be the truth, Socrates, and I admit that nobody desires evil.

B. *Plato,* Phaedo

It is not at all hard to understand my meaning, Socrates replied. If, for example, the one opposite, to go to sleep, existed without the corresponding opposite, to wake up, which is generated from the first, then all nature would at last make the tale of Endymion meaningless, and he would no longer be conspicuous; for everything else would be in the same state of sleep that he was in. And if all things were compounded together and never separated, the Chaos of Anaxagoras would soon be realized. Just in the same way, my dear Cebes, if all things in which there is any life were to die, and when they were dead were to remain in that form and not come to life again, would not the necessary result be that everything at last would be dead, and nothing alive? For if living things were generated from other sources than death, and were to die, the result is inevitable that all things would be consumed by death. Is it not so?

C. *Plato,* Theaetetus

SOCRATES: Then what shall we say, Theaetetus, if we are asked: 'But is what you describe possible for anyone? Can any man think what is not, either about something that is or absolutely?' I suppose we must answer to that: 'Yes, when he believes something and what he believes is not true.' Or what are we to say?
THEAETETUS: We must say that.
SOCRATES: Then is the same sort of thing possible in any other case?
THEAETETUS: What sort of thing?
SOCRATES: That a man should see something, and yet what he sees should be nothing.
THEAETETUS: No. How could that be?
SOCRATES: Yet surely if what he sees is something, it must be a thing that is. Or do you suppose that 'something' can be reckoned among things that have no being at all?
THEAETETUS: No, I don't.
SOCRATES: Then, if he sees something, he sees a thing that is.
THEAETETUS: Evidently.

SOCRATES:	And if he hears a thing, he hears something and hears a thing that is.
THEAETETUS:	Yes.
SOCRATES:	And if he touches a thing, he touches something, and if something, then a thing that is.
THEAETETUS:	That also is true.
SOCRATES:	And if he thinks, he thinks something, doesn't he?
THEAETETUS:	Necessarily.
SOCRATES:	And when he thinks something, he thinks a thing that is?
THEAETETUS:	I agree.
SOCRATES:	So to think what is not is to think nothing.
THEAETETUS:	Clearly.
SOCRATES:	But surely to think nothing is the same as not to think at all.
THEAETETUS:	That seems plain.
SOCRATES:	If so, it is impossible to think what is not, either about anything that is, or absolutely.

D. Aristotle, *Nichomachean Ethics*

Since there are evidently more than one end, and we choose some of these (e.g., wealth, flutes, and in general instruments) for the sake of something else, clearly not all ends are final ends; but the chief good is evidently something final. Therefore, if there is only one final end, this will be what we are seeking, and if there are more than one, the most final of these will be what we are seeking. Now we call that which is in itself worthy of pursuit more final than that which is worthy of pursuit for the sake of something else, and that which is never desirable for the sake of something else more final than the things that are desirable both in themselves and for the sake of that other thing, and therefore we call final without qualification that which is always desirable in itself and never for the sake of something else.

Now such a thing happiness, above all else, is held to be; for this we choose always for itself and never for the sake of something else, but honor, pleasure, reason, and every virtue we choose indeed for themselves (for if nothing resulted from them we should still choose each of them), but we choose them also for the sake of happiness, judging that by means of them we shall be happy. Happiness, on the other hand, no one chooses for the sake of these, nor, in general, for anything other than itself. . . .

Happiness, then, is something final and self-sufficient, and is [the chief good] and the end of action.

E. Augustine, **Confessions**

We speak of a long time and a short time, and we only say this of the past or future. For instance, we call a hundred years ago a long past time, and, likewise, a hundred years ahead a long future time.... But how is something long or short which does not exist? For, the past does not now exist and the future does not yet exist. So, let us not say: it *is* long; rather, let us say of past time: it *was* long; and of future: it *will be* long.

. . . Was that past time long in the sense that it was long when already past, or when it was still present? Of course it could have been long only at the time when that existed which was capable of being long, but as past it was already not existing; hence, it could not be long, for it was wholly nonexistent.

So let us not say past time was long; for we will discover nothing which could have been long, since, from the fact that it is past, it does not exist. Rather let us say: "That present time was long," for, when it was present, it was long. . . .

But . . . not even one day is present as a whole. It is made up of all twenty-four hours of night and day. The first of these regards the rest as future, the last one regards them as past; and the intermediate ones are to those preceding, as to the past; to those coming after, as to the future. And this one hour itself goes on by means of fleeting little parts: Whatever part of it has flown by is the past; whatever remains to it is the future. If one can conceive any part of time which could not be divided into even the most minute moments, then that alone is what may be called the present, and this flies over from the future into the past so quickly that it does not extend over the slightest instant. For if it has any extension, it is divided into past and future. But the present has no length.

Where then is the time which we may call long?

F. Anselm, Proslogion

And so, Lord, do thou, who dost give understanding to faith, give me so far as thou knowest it to be profitable, to understand that thou art as we believe; and that thou art that which we believe. And, indeed, we believe that thou art a being than which nothing greater can be conceived. Or is there no such nature, since the fool hath said in his heart, there is no God? (Psalms XIV.1). But, at any rate, this very fool, when he hears of this being of which I speak—a being than which nothing greater can be conceived—understands what he hears, and what he understands is in his understanding; although he does not understand it to exist.

. . . Hence, even the fool is convinced that something exists in the understanding, at least, than which nothing greater can be conceived. For, when he hears of this, he understands it. And whatever is understood, exists in the understanding. And assuredly that, than which nothing greater can be conceived, cannot exist in the understanding alone. For, suppose it exists in the understanding alone: then it can be conceived to exist in reality; which is greater.

Therefore, if that, than which nothing greater can be conceived, exists in the understanding alone, the very being, than which nothing greater can be conceived, is one, than which a greater can be conceived. But obviously this is impossible. Hence, there is no doubt that there exists a being, than which nothing greater can be conceived, and it exists both in the understanding and in reality.

G. Aquinas, Summa Theological

The second way [to prove the existence of God] is from the nature of efficient cause. In the world of sensible things we find there is an order of efficient causes. There is no case known (neither is it, indeed, possible) in which a thing is found to be the efficient cause of itself; for so it would be prior to itself, which is impossible. Now in efficient causes it is not possible to go on to infinity, because in all efficient causes following in order, the first is the cause of the intermediate cause, and the intermediate is the cause of the ultimate cause, whether the intermediate cause be several, or one only. Now to take away the cause is to take away the effect. Therefore, if there be no first cause among efficient causes, there will be no ultimate, nor any intermediate, cause. But if in efficient causes it is possible to go on to infinity, there will be no first efficient cause, neither will there be an ultimate effect, nor any intermediate efficient causes; all of which is plainly false. Therefore it is necessary to admit a first efficient cause, to which everyone gives the name of God.

H. Descartes, Meditations on First Philosophy

Nevertheless, I must remember that I am a man, and that consequently I am accustomed to sleep and in my dreams to imagine the same things that lunatics imagine when awake, or sometimes things which are even less plausible. How many times has it occurred that the quiet of the night made me dream of my usual habits: that I was here, clothed in a dressing gown, and sitting by the fire, although I was in fact lying undressed in bed! It seems apparent to me now, that I am not looking at this paper with my eyes closed, that this head that I shake is not drugged with sleep, that it is with design and deliberate intent that I stretch out this hand and perceive it. What happens in sleep seems not at all as clear and as distinct as all this. But I am speaking as though I never recall having been misled, while asleep, by similar illusions! When I consider these matters carefully, I realize so clearly that there are no conclusive indications by which waking life can be distinguished from sleep that I am quite astonished, and my bewilderment is such that it is almost able to convince me that I am sleeping.

I.1. Descartes, Meditations on First Philosophy

Since I know that all the things I conceive clearly and distinctly can be produced by God exactly as I conceive them, it is sufficient that I can clearly and distinctly conceive one thing apart from another to be certain that the one is distinct or different form the other. For they can be made to exist separately, at least by the omnipotence of God, and we are obliged to consider them different no matter what power produces this separation. From the very fact that I know with certainty that I exist, and that I find that absolutely nothing else belongs necessarily to my nature or essence except that I am a thinking being, I readily conclude that my essence consists solely in being a body which thinks or a substance whose whole essence or nature is only to think. And although perhaps . . . I have a body with which I am very closely united, nevertheless, since on the one hand I have a clear and distinct idea of myself insofar as I am only a thinking and not an extended being, and since on the other hand I have a distinct idea of body insofar as it is only an extended being which does not think, it is certain that this "I"—that is to say, my soul, by virtue of which I am what I am— is entirely and truly distinct from my body and that it can be or exist without it.

I.2. d'Holbach, **The System of Nature**

The beings of the human species . . . are susceptible of two sorts of motion: the one, that of the mass, by which an entire body, or some of its parts, are visibly transferred from one place to another; the other, internal and concealed, of some of which man is sensible, which so takes place without his knowledge and is not even to be guessed at but by the effect it outwardly produces. In a machine so extremely complex as man, formed by the combination of such a multiplicity of matter, so diversified in its properties, so different in its proportions, so varied in its modes of action, the motion necessarily becomes of the most complicated kind; its dullness, as well as its rapidi- ty, frequently escapes the observation of those themselves, in whom it takes place.

Let us not then be surprised, if when man would account to himself for his existence, for his manner of acting, finding so many obstacles to encounter,—he invented such strange hypotheses to explain the concealed spring of his machine— if when this motion appeared to him to be different from that of other bodies, he conceived an idea that he moved and acted in a manner altogether distinct from the other beings in nature. . . . He fell into the belief, that he perceived within himself a substance distinguished from that self, endowed with a secret force, in which he supposed existed qualities distinctly differing from those, of either the visible caus- es that acted on his organs, or those organs themselves. . . . Thus, for want of medi- tating nature—of considering her under her true point of view—of remarking the conformity—of noticing the simultaneity, the unity of the motion of this fancied motive-power with that of his body—of his material organs—he conjectured he was not only a distinct being but that he was set apart, with different energies, from all the other beings in nature; that he was of a more simple essence, having nothing in common with any thing by which he was surrounded; nothing that connected him with all that he beheld.

It is from thence has successively sprung his notions of *spirituality, immaterial- ity, immortality;* in short, all those vague unmeaning words, he has invented by degrees, in order to subtilize and designate the attributes of the unknown power, which he believes he contains within himself . . .

J. Locke, **An Essay Concerning Human Understanding**

This may show us wherein personal identity consists: not in the identity of sub- stance, but, as I have said, in the identity of consciousness, wherein if Socrates and the present mayor of Queinborough agree, they are the same person: if the same Socrates waking and sleeping do not partake of the same consciousness, Socrates waking and sleeping is not the same person. And to punish Socrates waking for what sleeping Socrates thought, and waking Socrates was never conscious of, would be no more of right, than to punish one twin for what his brother-twin did, whereof he knew nothing, because their outsides were so like that they could not be distinguished; for such twins have been seen.

K. Locke, *An Essay Concerning Human Understanding*

Words, by long and familiar use, . . . come to excite in men certain ideas so constantly and readily, that they are apt to suppose a natural connection between them. But that they signify only men's peculiar ideas, and that, *by a perfect arbitrary imposition,* is evident in that they often fail to excite in others (even that use the same language) the same ideas we take them to be signs of: and every man has so inviolable a liberty to make words stand for what ideas he pleases, that no one hath the power to make others have the same ideas in their minds that he has, when they use the same words that he does. . . . It is true, common use, by a tacit consent, appropriates certain sounds to certain ideas in all languages, which so far limits the signification of that sound, that unless a man applies it to the same idea, he does not speak properly: . . . But whatever be the consequence of any man's using of words differently, either from their general meaning, or the particular sense of the person to whom he addresses them; this is certain, their signification, in his use of them, is limited to his ideas, and they can be signs of nothing else.

L.1. Hume, A Treatise of Human Nature

For my part, when I enter most intimately into what I call *myself,* I always stumble on some particular perception or other, of heat or cold, light or shade, love or hatred, pain or pleasure. I never can catch *myself* at any time without a perception, and never can observe any thing but the perception. When my perceptions are removed for any time, as by sound sleep, so long am I insensible of *myself* and may truly be said not to exist. And were all my perceptions removed by death, and could I neither think, nor feel, nor see, nor love, nor hate after the dissolution of my body, I should be entirely annihilated, nor do I conceive what is farther requisite to make me a perfect nonentity. If any one upon serious and unprejudiced reflexion, thinks he has a different notion of *himself,* I must confess I can reason no longer with him. . . . He may, perhaps, perceive something simple and continued, which he calls *himself;* tho' I am certain there is no such principle in me.

But setting aside some metaphysicians of this kind, I may venture to affirm of the rest of mankind that they are nothing but a bundle of collections of different perceptions, which succeed each other with an inconceivable rapidity, and are in a perpetual flux and movement. . . . The mind is a kind of theatre, where several perceptions successively make their appearances; pass, re-pass, glide away, and mingle in an infinite variety of postures and situations. There is properly no *simplicity* in it at one time, nor *identity* in different; whatever natural propension we may have to imagine that simplicity and identity. The comparison of the theatre must not mislead us. They are the successive perceptions only, that constitute the mind; nor have we the most distant notion of the place where these scenes are represented, or the materials of which it is composed.

L.2. *Reid,* **Essays on the Intellectual Powers of Man**

My personal identity . . . implies the continued existence of that indivisible thing which I call myself. Whatever this self may be, it is something which thinks, and deliberates, and resolves, and acts, and suffers. My thoughts, and actions, and feelings, change every moment; they have no continued, but a successive, existence; but that self, or I, to which they belong, is permanent, and has the same relation to all the succeeding thoughts, actions, and feelings which I call mine. . . .

The proper evidence I have of all this is remembrance. I remember that twenty years ago I conversed with such a person; I remember several things that passed in that conversation; my memory testifies not only that this was done, but that it was done by me who now remembers it. If it was done by me, I must have existed at that time, and continued to exist from that time to the present: if the identical person whom I call myself had not a part in that conversation, my memory is fallacious; it gives a distinct and positive testimony of what is not true. Every man in his senses believes what he distinctly remembers, and everything he remembers convinces him that he existed at the time remembered.

M.1. *Locke, letter to the Bishop of Worcester*

"Everything that has a beginning must have a cause" is a true principle of reason, or a proposition certainly true; which we come to know by . . . contemplating our ideas and perceiving that the idea of beginning to be is necessarily connected with the ideas of some operation; and the idea of operation with the idea of something operating, which we call a cause. And so the beginning to be is perceived to agree with the idea of a cause, as is expressed in the proposition, and thus it comes to be a certain proposition, and so may be called a principle of reason, as every true proposition is to him that perceives the certainty of it.

M.2. *Hume,* **A Treatise of Human Nature**

'Tis a general maxim in philosophy, that "Whatever begins to exist, must have cause of existence." This is commonly taken for granted, in all reasonings, without any proof given or demanded. . . .

But here is an argument, which proves at once that the foregoing proposition is neither intuitively nor demonstrably certain. We can never demonstrate the necessity of a cause to every new existence, or new modification of existence, without showing, at the same time, the impossibility there is that any thing can ever begin to exist without some productive principle; and where the latter proposition cannot be proved, we must despair of ever being able to prove the former. Now that the latter proposition is utterly incapable of a demonstrative proof, we may satisfy ourselves by considering that, as all distinct ideas are separable from each other, and as the ideas of cause and effect are evidently distinct, 'twill be easy for us to conceive any object to be nonexistent this moment, and existent the next, without conjoining to it the distinct idea of a cause or productive principle. The separation, therefore, of the idea of a cause from that of a beginning of existence, is plainly possible for the imagination; and consequently, the actual separation of these objects is so far possible, that it implies no contradiction nor absurdity; and is therefore incapable of being refuted by any reasoning from mere ideas; without which 'tis impossible to demonstrate the necessity of a cause.

Accordingly we shall find upon examination, that every demonstration, which has been produced for the necessity of a cause, is fallacious and sophistical.

N. Mill, Utilitarianism

The only proof capable of being given that an object is visible, is that people actually see it; the only proof that a sound is audible, is that people hear it: and so of the other sources of our experience. In like manner, I apprehend, the sole evidence it is possible to produce that any thing is desirable, is that people do actually desire it. If the end which the utilitarian doctrine proposes to itself were not, in theory and in practice, acknowledged to be an end, nothing could ever convince any person that it was so. No reason can be given why the general happiness is desirable, except that each person, so far as he believes it to be attainable, desires his own happiness. This, however, being a fact, we have not only all the proof which the case admits of, but all which it is possible to require, that happiness is a good; that each person's happiness is a good to that person; and the general happiness, therefore, a good to the aggregate of all persons. Happiness has made out its titles as *one* of the ends of conduct, and consequently one of the criteria of morality.

O. Russell, The Problems of Philosophy

It is sometimes said that 'light *is* a form of wave-motion,' but this is misleading, for the light which we immediately see, which we known directly by means of our senses, is *not* a form of wave-motion, but something quite different—something which we all know if we are not blind, though we cannot describe it so as to convey our knowledge to a man who is blind. A wave-motion, on the contrary, could quite well be described to a blind man, since he can acquire a knowledge of space by the sense of touch; and he can experience a wave-motion by a sea voyage almost as well as we can. But this, which a blind man can understand, is not what we mean by *light;* we mean by *light* just that which a blind man can never understand, and which we can never describe to him.

P. Russell, The Problems of Philosophy

Consider such a proposition as 'Edinburgh is north of London.' Here we have a relation between two places, and it seems plain that the relation subsists independently of our knowledge of it. When we come to know that Edinburgh is north of London, we come to know something which has only to do with Edinburgh and London: we do not cause the truth of the proposition by coming to know it, on the contrary we merely apprehend a fact which was there before we knew it. The part of the earth's surface where Edinburgh stands would be north of the part where London stands, even if there were no human beings to know about north and south, and even if there were no minds at all in the universe. . . .

This conclusion, however, is met by the difficulty that the relation 'north of' does not seem to *exist* in the same sense in which Edinburgh and London exist. If we ask 'Where and when does this relation exist?' the answer must be 'Nowhere and nowhen.' There is no place or time where we can find this relation 'north of'. It does not exist in Edinburgh any more than in London, for it relates the two and is neutral as between them. Nor can we say that it exists at any particular time. Now everything that can be apprehended by the senses or by introspection exists at some particular time. Hence the relation 'north of' is radically different from such things. It is neither in space nor in time, neither material nor mental; yet it is something.

Q. C. S. Lewis, Miracles

We may in fact state it as a rule that "No thought is valid if it can be fully explained as the result of irrational causes." Every reader of this book applies this rule automatically all day long. When a sober man tells you that the house is full of rats or snakes, you attend to him: if you know that his belief in the rats and snakes is due to *delirium tremens* you do not even bother to look for them. If you even *suspect* an irrational cause, you begin to pay less attention to a man's beliefs; your friend's pessimistic view of the European situation alarms you less when you discover that he is suffering from a bad liver attack. Conversely, when we discover a belief to be false we then first look about for irrational causes ("I was tired"—"I was in a hurry"—"I wanted to believe it"). . . . All thoughts which are so caused are valueless. We never, in our ordinary thinking, admit any exceptions to this rule.

Now it would clearly be preposterous to apply this rule to each particular thought as we come to it and yet not to apply it to all thoughts taken collectively, that is, to human reason as a whole. Each particular thought is valueless if it is the result of irrational causes. Obviously, then, the whole process of human thought, what we call Reason, is equally valueless if it is the result of irrational causes. Hence every theory of the universe which makes the human mind a result of irrational causes is inadmissible, for it would be a proof that there are no such things as proofs. Which is nonsense.

But Naturalism, as commonly held, is precisely a theory of this sort. The mind, like every other particular thing or event, is supposed to be simply the product of the Total System. It is supposed to be that and nothing more, to have no power whatever of "going on its own accord." And the Total System is not supposed to be rational. All thoughts whatever are therefore the results of irrational causes, and nothing more than that.

R.1. Moore, Principia Ethica

In fact, if it is not the case that 'good' denotes something simple and indefinable, only two alternatives are possible: either it is a complex, a given whole, about the correct analysis of which there may be disagreement; or else it means nothing at all. . . .

The hypothesis that disagreement about the meaning of good is disagreement with regard to the correct analysis of a given whole, may be most plainly seen to be incorrect by consideration of the fact that, whatever definition be offered, it may be always asked, with significance, of the complex so defined, whether it is itself good. To take, for instance, one of the more plausible, because one of the more complicated, of such proposed definitions, it may easily be thought, at first sight, that to be good may mean to be that which we desire to desire. Thus if we apply this definition to a particular instance and say 'When we think that A is good, we are thinking that A is one of the things which we desire to desire,' our proposition may seem quite plausible. But, if we carry the investigating further, and ask ourselves 'Is it good to desire to desire A?' it is apparent, on a little reflection, that this question is itself as intelligible, as the original question 'Is A good?'—that we are, in fact, now asking for exactly the same information about the desire to desire A, for which we formerly asked with regard to A itself. . . .

And the same consideration is sufficient to dismiss the hypothesis that 'good' has no meaning whatsoever. . . . Whoever will attentively consider with himself what is actually before his mind when he asks the question 'Is pleasure (or whatever it may be) after all good?' can easily satisfy himself that he is not merely wondering whether pleasure is pleasant. . . . Everyone does in fact understand the question 'Is this good?' When he thinks of it, his state of mind is different from what it would be, were he asked 'Is this pleasant, or desired, or approved?' It has a distinct meaning for him, even though he may not recognize in what respect it is distinct. . . .

'Good,' then, is indefinable.

R.2. Ayer, **Language, Truth, and Logic**

We being by admitting that the fundamental ethical concepts are unanalysable, inasmuch as there is no criterion by which one can test the validity of the judgments in which they occur. So far we are in agreement with the absolutists. But, unlike the absolutists, we are able to give an explanation of this fact about ethical concepts. We say that the reason why they are unanalysable is that they are mere pseudo-concepts. The presence of an ethical symbol in a proposition adds nothing to its factual content. Thus if I say to someone, "You acted wrongly in stealing that money," I am not stating anything more than if I had simply said, "You stole that money." In adding that this action is wrong I am not making any further statement about it. I am simply evincing my moral disapproval of it. It is as if I had said, "You stole that money," in a peculiar tone of horror, or written it with the addition of some special exclamation marks. The tone, or the exclamation marks, adds nothing to the literal meaning of the sentence. It merely serves to show that the expression of it is attended by certain feelings in the speaker.

S.1. Ayer, **The Problem of Knowledge**

For example, I am now seated in a vineyard: and I can fairly claim to know that there are clusters of grapes a few feet away from me. But in making even such a simple statement as 'that is a bunch of grapes,' a statement so obvious that in ordinary conversation, as opposed, say, to an English lesson, it would never be made, I am in a manner going beyond my evidence. I can see the grapes: but it is requisite also that in the appropriate conditions I should be able to touch them. They are not real grapes if they are not tangible; and from the fact that I am having just these visual experiences, it would seem that nothing logically follows about what I can or cannot touch. Neither is it enough that I can see and touch the grapes: other people must be able to perceive them too. If I had reason to believe that no one else could, in the appropriate conditions, see or touch them, I should be justified in concluding that I was undergoing a hallucination. Thus, while my basis for making this assertion may be very strong, so strong indeed as to warrant a claim to knowledge, it is not conclusive; my experience, according to this argument, could still be what it is even though the grapes which I think that I am perceiving really do exist.

S.2. *Austin,* Sense and Sensibilia

If I watch for some time an animal a few feet in front of me, in a good light, if I prod it perhaps, sniff, and take note of the noises it makes, I may say, 'That's a pig'; and this too will be 'incorrigible,' nothing could be produced that would show that I had made a mistake. . . .

The situation in which I would properly be said to have *evidence* for the statement that some animal is a pig is that, for example, in which the beast itself it not actually on view, but I can see plenty of pig-like marks on the ground outside its retreat. If I find a few buckets of pig-food, that's a bit more evidence, and the noises and the smell may provide better evidence still. But if the animal then emerges and stands there plainly in view, but there is no longer any question of collecting evidence; its coming into view doesn't provide me with more *evidence* that it's a pig, I can now just *see* that it is, the question is settled.

Notes to the Passages

A. Plato, *Meno*, in *The Dialogues of Plato* trans. Benjamin Jowett, 4th ed. 1953 (Oxford University Press).

B. Plato, *Phaedo*, trans. F. J. Church (Indianapolis and New York: Bobbs-Merrill, 1951), p. 19.

C. Plato, *Theaetetus*, in Francis M. Cornford, *Plato's Theory of Knowledge* (New Jersey: Humanities Press Inc., 1957), pp. 114–15.

D. Aristotle, *Nichomachean Ethics* (1097a, b), in Richard McKeon, *The Basic Works of Aristotle* (New York: Random House, 1941), pp. 941–42.

E. Augustine, *Confessions* (Bk. 11, Chaps. 14–15), trans. Vernon J. Bourke, Fathers of the Church Series, Vol. 5 (Washington, D.C.: Catholic University of America Press, 1953), pp. 343–46.

F. Anselm, *Proslogion* (Chap. II), trans. S. N. Deane. Reprinted by permission of The Open Court Publishing Company (1961 edition; introduction by Charles Hartshorne), LaSalle, Illinois.

G. Thomas Aquinas, *Summa Theological* (Part I, Q2, Art 3), in A. C. Pegis, *Introduction to St. Thomas Aquinas* (New York: Random House, 1948), pp. 25–26.

H. René Descartes, *Meditations on First Philosophy*, trans. Laurence J. Laffleur (Indianapolis and New York: Bobbs-Merrill, 1960), pp. 18–19.

I.1. Descartes, *Meditations*, pp. 73–74.

1.2. Baron Paul d'Holbach, *The System of Nature*, trans. H. D. Robinson (New York: Burt Franklin, 1970), Chap. VI.

J. John Locke, *An Essay Concerning Human Understanding*, Vol. 1 (II, xxvii, 1g), (New York: Dover, 1959), p. 460.

K. Locke, *Essay*, Vol. 2 (III, ii, 8), p. 12.

L.1 David Hume, *A Treatise of Human Nature* (I, iv, 6), ed. L. A. Selby-Bigge (London: Oxford University Press, 1888), pp. 252–53.

L.2 Thomas Reid, *Essays on the Intellectual Powers of Man* (III, 4) ed. A. D. Woozley (London: Macmillan, 1941), p. 203.

M.1. John Locke, letter to the Right Rev. Edward Lord Bishop of Worcester, in *Works* Vol. 4 (London, 1812), pp. 61–62.

M.2. Hume, *Treatise*, (I, iii, 3), pp. 78–80.

N. John Stuart Mill, *Utilitarianism*, in Marshall Cohen, *The Philosophy of John Stuart Mill* (New York: Random House, 1961), p. 363.

O. Bertrand Russell, *The Problems of Philosophy* (New York: Oxford University Press, 1959), p. 28.

P. Russell, *The Problems of Philosophy*, pp. 97–98.

Q. C. S. Lewis, *Miracles* (New York: Macmillan, 1947), pp. 20–22.

R.1.   G. E. Moore, *Principia Ethica* (London: Cambridge University Press, 1903), pp. 15–17.

R.2.   A. J. Ayer, *Language, Truth, and Logic* (New York: Dover, 1952), p. 107.

S.1.   A. J. Ayer, *The Problem of Knowledge* (Baltimore: Penguin, 1956), pp. 56–57.

S.2.   J. L. Austin, *Sense and Sensibilia* (London: Oxford University Press, 1962), pp. 114–15.